THE TRANSFER OF POWER
IN SOUTH AFRICA

einige Bleistift —
stoerige

CapeTown, März 2001

President F.W. de Klerk and Nelson Mandela, August 1991: The agony of courageous statemanship. (Photograph by Rodger Bosch)

THE TRANSFER OF POWER IN SOUTH AFRICA

T.R.H. DAVENPORT

David Philip Publishers
Cape Town

Published in southern Africa 1998 by David Philip Publishers (Pty) Ltd, 208 Werdmuller Centre, Newry Street, Claremont, South Africa 7700
First published in North America 1998 by University of Toronto Press Inc., Toronto, Buffalo, London

ISBN 0 86486 410 8

Printed in South Africa by National Book Printers, Drukkery Street, Goodwood, South Africa

Contents

PREFACE vii

TIME LINE xi

ABBREVIATIONS xv

1 Breaking Through 1

2 Peacemaking 25

3 Constitution Making 47

4 The Growing Pains of Democracy, 1994–1997 79

NOTES 107

INDEX 139

Maps appear on pages 66–9.

Archbishop Tutu, chair of the Truth and Reconciliation Commission, handles the problems of the national conscience (see page 100). (Cartoon by Zapiro. *Argus*, 25 April 1996)

Preface

It would be difficult to live in South Africa during the 1990s without sensing, in one way or another, that the unexpected has happened, that instead of heading, as one prime minister put it, towards 'a future too ghastly to contemplate,' we have suddenly been led through a gap into the sunlight, emerging as one people rather than a multiplicity of peoples, sharing common symbols of flag and anthem, and regaining the respect, even at times the affection, of a world that until recently was disposed to be hostile.

The realities are not quite as rosy as this. The tasks ahead look, to normal rational minds, quite impossible. South Africa remains one of the most violent and corrupt countries in the world. There are deep rifts of incomprehension between our many communities. Most of us do not understand the languages of the rest of us, a knowledge of three of our eleven languages being exceptional. There is much poverty and unemployment; far too many of our people are too untrained to come within range even of subsistence wages; and the passage from that wonder year of 1990 has been far from easy.

So it was a challenge to write these lectures. Historians in general are most at home when dealing with events that have been allowed to settle over time. That luxury was not to be had in this instance. But I have profited from advice from informed colleagues and friends, notably Hugh Corder, Willie Hofmeyr, Jeremy Sarkin, Christopher Saunders, Dene Smuts, and Peter Vale, who read the typescript but should not be held to account for any errors that have survived their scrutiny. The learned monographs are beginning to arrive – though not yet in significant numbers – and I have profited from the work of Doreen Atkinson, Steven Friedman, and Andrew Reynolds in particular. I also want to pay tribute to the quality of the work displayed by a number of journalists, some of whom are mentioned in the endnotes, for their coverage of events which often posed difficulties of comprehension and sometimes involved personal risk, above all when it was necessary to report state actions that were in breach of the law; hence my frequent references to individual journalists in the endnotes – but I must stress that the list could have been longer. As well, my thanks go to cartoonists Tony Grogan and Jonathan Shapiro, both of whom have contributed richly to this volume.

I also wish to thank friends and colleagues in the Department of History at the University of Western Ontario for having invited me to give these lectures, especially Neville Thompson, who made things possible for me, and the department's secretarial staff, who made them easy. And very special thanks go to Edwin A. Goodman, father of the late Joanne Goodman, in whose memory the lectures were dedicated, for his generosity and his supportive presence during what I chiefly remember as a festive week.

These pages contain a revised version of the lectures, which I gave at the University of Western Ontario between 26 and 28 September 1995 and which have been updated to take into account developments that have occurred since then. The first two chapters cover the ground of the first two lectures. The third is focused on constitutional changes just as the third lecture was, but it now extends beyond the Interim Constitution of

1993–4 to take in the creation of the new Constitution of the Republic of South Africa, which came into force in February 1997 after certification by the new Constitutional Court. The final chapter, which is largely new, looks at the record of the Government of National Unity, formed under Nelson Mandela's presidency in May 1994, and traces events through to 1997.

Rodney Davenport
Cape Town, September 1997

Time Line

1960	Sharpeville crisis. First republican constitution.
1964	'Rivonia' trial: Mandela and others imprisoned for life
1976–7	Soweto crisis
1978–89	P.W. Botha state president
1983	Botha's three-chamber republican constitution excludes Africans
1985	Botha's 'Rubicon' speech
1986	Commonwealth Eminent Persons' Group visit
	Mass Democratic Movement emerges
1989 Aug.–Sept.	F.W. de Klerk ousts P.W. Botha
	White general election
1990 Jan.–Feb.	Mandela-de Klerk talks, and release of Mandela
1991 Jan.	Mandela offers two-stage talks (Breakthrough 1)
Dec.	CODESA meeting at Kempton Park: negotiations begin
1992 Mar.	White referendum: a two-thirds majority for reform

	May	CODESA breaks down
	June	Boipatong massacre brings ANC rolling mass action
	Sept.	ANC's failed Ciskei coup; but NP and ANC draw up Record of Understanding
	Oct.	Slovo's sunset clause (Breakthrough 2)
1993	Apr.	Murder of Chris Hani; but
	Apr.–June	ANC and NP agree on 27 Apr. 1994 election
		AWB invades World Trade Centre
	July	Adoption of thirty-three constitutional principles
	Nov.–Dec.	Interim Constitution completed
1994	Mar.	Fall of Mangope (Bophuthatswana) and Gqozo (Ciskei)
		Shell House massacre, Johannesburg
	Apr.	First democratic general election
	May	Inauguration of President Mandela and formation of the Government of National Unity
		National Unity and Reconciliation Bill
	June	South Africa rejoins Commonwealth
	Aug.	South Africa joins Southern African Development Community
	Oct.	Reconstruction and Development Programme launched
		South Africa returns to the United Nations
1995	Feb.	Green paper on land reform
		Labour Relations Bill published
	Mar.	De Kock trial begins
	Nov.	Local government elections (May 1996 in W. Cape and KwaZulu-Natal)
1996	Mar.	Malan trial begins
	Apr.	Truth and Reconciliation Commission

		opens hearings
1996	May	Adoption of new constitution by the Constitutional Assembly
		National Party leaves Government of National Unity
	July	RDP transferred to Vice-President Thabo Mbeki
	Sept.	Constitutional Court refers new constitution back to Constitutional Assembly
	Oct.	Exoneration of Malan and conviction of de Kock
	Dec.	President Mandela signs new constitution
		Amnesty date extended to 10 May 1997
1997	Feb.	Parliament opens. Constitution adopted
	Mar.	Manuel's GEAR budget
	May	De Klerk presents NP case to TRC
		Mbeki presents ANC case to TRC
	Aug.	Conviction and amnesty for Coetzee
		Hani hearing before amnesty committee
	Sept.	Biko, Goniwe, and PEBCO hearings before amnesty committee
		De Klerk's retirement from politics

The restoration of land rights. Derek Hanekom, minister of land affairs, attempts surgery for a chronic complaint (see pages 86–7). (Cartoon by Zapiro. *Mail and Guardian*, 10 November 1994)

Abbreviations

ANC	African National Congress
APLA	Azanian People's Liberation Army (linked to the PAC)
AWB	Afrikaner Weerstandsbeweging (Afrikaner Resistance Movement)
AZANLA	Azanian National Liberation Army (linked to AZAPO)
AZAPO	Azanian People's Organization
CCB	Civil Cooperation Bureau
CODESA	Convention for a Democratic South Africa
CONTRALESA	Congress [Council] of Traditional Leaders
COSAG	Concerned South Africans Group
COSATU	Congress of South African Trade Unions
CP	Conservative Party
DP	Democratic Party
EPG	(Commonwealth) Eminent Persons' Group
FF	Freedom Front
GNU	Government of National Unity
IDASA	Institute for a Democratic South Africa
IEC	Independent Electoral Commission
IFP	Inkatha Freedom Party
MDM	Mass Democratic Movement

MK	Umkhonto we Sizwe [Spear of the Nation] (ANC militia)
NCOP	National Council of Provinces
NEDLAC	National Economic Development & Labour Advisory Council
NP	National Party
NPKF	National Peace-Keeping Force
PAC	Pan-Africanist Congress
PEBCO	Port Elizabeth Black Community Organization
RDP	Reconstruction and Development Programme
SABC	South African Broadcasting Corporation
SACP	South African Communist Party
SADF	South African Defence Force
SANDF	South African National Defence Force
SAP	South African Police
SAPS	South African Police Service
TBVC states	Transkei, Bophuthatswana, Venda, Ciskei (independent homelands)
TEC	Transitional Executive Council
TRC	Truth and Reconciliation Commission
UDF	United Democratic Front

1

Breaking Through

MACHIAVELLI PROCLAIMED IN HIS *Discourses* that when faced with a crucial political choice, humankind invariably chooses the least sensible course, which also appears at the time to be the most heroic.[1] He was not always right about this. The story told in these pages is one in which abrasive words and violent actions that might have been expected to plunge a demoralized country into civil war were often used by people of vision to kick-start a new stage of a difficult negotiating process. So far, this has gone on for seven years. During this time, South Africa has changed from being the world's polecat to being a potential polestar.

This first chapter is concerned with the story of how the process that came to life with the release of Nelson Mandela from jail in February 1990 led to his election as president in May 1994. The second chapter will look at the bumpy process of reconciliation between the rival elements, without which no constitution, however well contrived, could be expected to hold the new nation together for any meaningful period of time. The third will handle the steps leading to the adoption of South Africa's first legitimate constitution at the end of 1996. And chapter 4, which formed no part of the original lecture series, will handle developments under the Government of National Unity as it tried, during the same period, to move from a peacemaking to a nation-building posture in an attempt to master the enormous problems of transition to an open, democratic society.

Change without a violent revolution did not seem possible in the 1980s. Endemic racism and repression had poisoned the apartheid years. Apartheid had not been systematically applied until the 1960s and was on the way out by the mid-1970s, but most countries of the world were voting against South Africa in the United Nations General Assembly, were cutting it off from funds, trade, and weaponry, or arming its opponents in exile. Unemployment was rising. The range and intensity of internal resistance was spreading, despite a four-year state of emergency from 1986. Bastions of white supremacy in Mozambique and Rhodesia had fallen; South-West Africa was on the way to becoming the independent state of Namibia; and in the course of resisting what the government referred to as 'total onslaught,' South Africa was moving fast towards bankruptcy.

Economic Catastrophes and Political Windfalls

It was the historian C.W. de Kiewiet who coined the famous aphorism that South Africa had advanced politically by catastrophes and economically by windfalls. Since 1985 the reverse may have been the case. A near collapse of the South African economy from outside pressures was relieved by the politico-economic breakdown of Eastern Europe, which the country's rulers had imagined to be their main source of danger. The fortuitous timing of these events not only made President Reagan's policy of 'constructive engagement' in Africa viable, but it enabled a few talented politicians to work wonders in a very 'rough neighbourhood.' Especially valuable were the efforts of (in alphabetical order) President Fidel Castro of Cuba (despite his resistance to the Gorbachev 'thaw'); Chester Crocker, Reagan's assistant secretary of state for African affairs, who managed to separate a dogfight between the beleaguered white South African forces and the black liberators; F.W. de Klerk, the right-wing Transvaler president of South Africa, who was prepared and actually able to make his National Party disown its past to face a different kind of future; and Nelson Mandela, the African National Congress (ANC) leader who had entered jail in 1962 as a political firebrand of massive integrity and who survived a twenty-seven-year incarceration, with hard labour, to emerge – on de Klerk's decision – with his leadership qualities unimpaired, his anger under control, and his integrity intact. The collective statesmanship of these men in particular invites the suggestion that these were years in which human wisdom was strong enough in respect of southern Africa to opt for the sensible rather than the heroic and – despite Machiavelli's terrifying observation – actually to win through.

It had been widely accepted from at least the mid-1970s that 'separate development' in South Africa was a nonstarter. The government had begun to cut away at petty apartheid (in the form of such objects as separate park benches and post office counters) in the belief that this would make the citadel of grand apartheid (large-scale territorial and political separation) easier to defend. But the Soweto crisis of 1976–7, when nearly every black and Coloured township broke down in anarchy, led to the removal of some key apartheid laws, including the Urban Areas and Bantu Education Acts, even though not all their provisions were scrapped and state repression continued unabated. Even P.W. Botha, president from 1978 to 1989, for all his destabilization of the frontier and his refusal to take risks, at least saw the need for reform.

Members of the ANC and the South African Communist Party (SACP), after enduring a stressful alliance in exile or in jail during the 1960s and 1970s, were in no mood to conciliate a government that had shown so little desire to talk. In conferences at Morogoro, Tanzania, in 1969 and Kabwe, Zambia, in 1985,[2] ANC talk had centred mainly on the struggle. Not until the Organization of African Unity conference at Harare, Zimbabwe, in August 1989 was there a conditional offer of negotiation, though the ANC executive had discussed such an option in a published statement on 9 October 1987.[3]

Chance encounters between key people had helped to bring about these changes, even though – as Christopher Saunders has carefully explained – there were other ANC-initiated processes going on at the same time.[4] Allister Sparks tells how Pieter de Waal and Kobie Coetsee were tennis partners at the University of the Orange Free State in the 1950s. They remained friends. Pieter became a lawyer at Brandfort, and Kobie rose to become minister of justice, police, and prisons in the South African government. Winnie Mandela was exiled to Brandfort in 1977, and when she needed a lawyer she approached Pieter, the only lawyer in town. Pieter protested but was told to help her. His wife Adèle became friendly with Winnie, and when Winnie got into trouble with the police, Pieter asked Minister Kobie to have her banning order reviewed and, later, even to consider her husband's release. In 1985 Nelson Mandela was hospitalized, and Winnie happened to be on the same plane to Cape Town as Kobie. They chatted.[5] Four years of secret high-level talks followed, in the course of which Mandela and Kobie Coetsee found each other. Kobie made it possible for Mandela's lawyer, George Bizos, to make contact with the ANC leaders in Lusaka in order to synchronize their efforts. This contact, once made, was kept up through the ingenuity of a very resourceful ANC leader in Durban, Mac Maharaj.[6]

Knowing that President Botha was considering the release of Mandela but on terms which the latter could not accept, Coetsee worked to keep communications open. Soon afterwards, at a Commonwealth summit in the Bahamas in 1986, an Eminent Persons' Group (EPG) was appointed to visit South Africa to take the discussions further. The members of the group were allowed to meet Mandela, who greatly impressed them,[7] and they were making good progress when, at a critical moment, Botha seems to have been convinced by his security chiefs that the negotiations were dangerous, and ordered air raids on ANC bases in the frontline states, thus torpedoing the talks and sending the EPG racing home.[8] But Mandela would not let Botha off the hook. He pressed for a meeting, with support from Niël Barnard, head of the National Intelligence Service, and Barnard's persistence brought the two together at the Tuynhuys, the presidential office in Cape Town, on 5 July 1989. But the ever-suspicious Botha demanded from Mandela a public renunciation of violence, which the latter simply could not make.[9] Fortunately, the ANC leaders in Lusaka had by then built up very good links both inside South Africa and elsewhere in the world.[10] Many prominent South African business leaders, clerics, opposition MPs, and students and staff from the University of Stellenbosch (the hub of the Afrikaner establishment) had ignored Botha's order to stay at home. Even Piet de Lange, head of the influential Afrikaner Broederbond, who had received a cutting ANC riposte at a public dinner in New York, was persuaded by Thabo Mbeki to build on the relationship rather than break it.[11] The government and the ANC were now really talking to each other.

P.W. Botha had wrecked international confidence with his disastrous 'crossing-the-Rubicon' speech in 1985, when he had surprised world opinion by taking a defiant isolationist stance after leading everyone to expect an announcement of major reforms.[12] His continued intransigence in his talks with Mandela meant that he simply had to go before any real progress could be made. He fell from power in August 1989 after a well-staged cabinet coup, which had been preceded by some bitter cabinet infighting and was led by F.W. de Klerk.

Botha's replacement by de Klerk did not in itself herald a change of direction. De Klerk was a clever politician and one without leftward leanings. He claimed not to have had a 'road to Damascus' conversion, though his Dopper (puritanical) sensibilities had been moved by the sermon at his inauguration, and he was open to the arguments of his liberal journalist brother, Willem. Yet F.W. persistently held that apartheid had been a 'good try,' which unfortunately had failed. In public, he would not call it immoral. He had openly supported the system, and despite his explicit professions of innocence, he has not escaped repeated attempts to link him with abuses of human rights, notably in statements given before the Truth and Reconciliation Commission that was appointed in 1995.[13] He was at least anxious to hold his right wing in check. It certainly needed protection for its past record. It was in a position to cause him a lot of trouble if not protected, and a premature acceptance of complicity in the skulduggery of apartheid could have made it too dangerous for de Klerk to carry his followers into what could only be an area of considerable political risk.[14]

It was his actions, though, that mattered. September 1989 was not an easy time to take power, with a general election due that very month and the government in disarray. Not surprisingly, the party fared worse in these elections than it had in any election since 1953, though it just held on to a narrow majority over all opposition parties. Vested with presidential powers, de Klerk removed Botha's securocrats from their position of control in the cabinet, replacing them with a security system of his own. But he allowed public debate to open up, set several prominent Robben Islanders free, including the elderly Walter Sisulu, and in December summoned the cabinet to a *bosberaad* (the first of many 'councils in the bush') to thrash out a new strategy through which the National Party (NP) could place itself at the head of reform while retaining a firm hold on power. Yet he kept his reform strategy for the forthcoming parliamentary session almost entirely to himself.

These actions alone could not break the ice with the ANC, whose posture remained firm on the immediate need to build a democratic, nonracial South Africa. But de Klerk had already received a challenge from Mandela as a result of the talks Mandela had been allowed to hold with leaders of the Mass Democratic Movement in early December 1989.[15] When the two men met on 12 and 13 December at the Tuynhuys, Mandela again rejected demands that the ANC should unilaterally abandon the armed struggle and its association with the SACP, and insisted that its demand for majority rule in a nonracial state would have to be faced. To this end he proposed a two-stage process: first, a meeting on how to create a proper climate for negotiations; second, the negotiations themselves. He noted that de Klerk was paying attention and saw this as a sign that the president was 'a man we could do business with,' even if de Klerk subsequently caused him doubts.[16] De Klerk apparently gave Mandela privileged access to the speech he was to make in Parliament on 2 February 1990.[17] On that important occasion he assured the members that they were still the lawful legislature of South Africa; but after referring obliquely to the need to abandon violence and to learn a lesson from the collapse of the communist economies, he announced his intention to go for real negotiations with the African leadership. He said he would unban the ANC, the SACP, the Pan-Africanist Congress (PAC), and other restricted bodies, repeal the emergency regulations, and open up public debate; he would also release Mandela without conditions. This took his party and Parliament by surprise.

Mandela was released on 11 February from the Victor Verster prison in Paarl after spending some weeks almost literally as a guest of the state. His unpunctual but dignified walk to freedom, in company with his wife, Winnie, and his appearance on the balcony of the Cape Town city hall to address the crowd on the same evening became occasions of ecstatic rejoicing, with a little public hooliganism thrown in.

Then began the great unwind. The exiled leaders of the ANC were allowed to return to South Africa under a promise of safe conduct, and in early May they held talks with the government at Groote Schuur, the president's official residence, to deal with the release of political prisoners and the general return of exiles. In August Mandela announced a unilateral ending of the armed struggle, though the ANC's military wing, Umkhonto we Sizwe (Spear of the Nation, 'MK') remained in existence. Then, in October, de Klerk lifted all remaining restrictions under the five-year state of emergency.[18] In January 1991 Mandela repeated his call for an all-party congress to prepare for a constituent assembly, to which the government agreed the following month – a moment that Steven Friedman has called the breakthrough.[19] Still asserting itself as the legal holder of power, the government then set about repeating the surviving segregationist laws.[20]

A Convention for a Democratic South Africa

The year 1991 was a cat-and-mouse time in which the two sides sized each other up against a background of continuing unrest. At the end of it, in fulfilment of the Mandela–de Klerk proposals, a Convention for a Democratic South Africa (CODESA) met at the World Trade Centre, Kempton Park, on 20 and 21 December.[21] The convention was attended by representatives of eight mainstream political parties, including the Inkatha Freedom Party from KwaZulu, and by most homeland administrations but by none of the white or black right-wing ultra-nationalist bodies. This theatrical occasion was opened by the white chief justice, Michael Corbett, and presided over by two other judges of different cultural backgrounds. Dedicatory prayers were offered by Christian, Jewish, and Muslim religious leaders, after which the parties and other public figures present made formal statements in an agreed sequence.

All went swimmingly until de Klerk, who had been granted the right to speak last, picked that moment to berate the ANC for not having disbanded Umkhonto we Sizwe (despite Mandela's formal renunciation of the armed struggle the previous year). Mandela was furious. He strode to the microphone and harangued the president for pursuing a double agenda, accusing him of negotiating in public while secretly encouraging units in the security forces to destablilize the ANC.[22] The clash was dramatic enough. Its impact, though, may not have been entirely negative; for it dispelled any notion that NP-ANC collusion lay behind the conference while highlighting these two parties as the pace-setters in the negotiations. The rivals made suitable amends the next day, and the event did not prevent CODESA from issuing what Sparks has called a 'sweepingly liberal' declaration of intent, followed by the setting up of five working groups to prepare the ground for a nonracial democratic form of government.[23]

When de Klerk opened Parliament on 24 January 1992, he gave CODESA's decisions positive endorsement but stressed that any major changeover would require 'a referendum in which every South African will be able to take part and in which the result may be determined globally as well as per parliamentary voters' rolls.' He knew that the gulf between the NP and the ANC was much wider than the general consensus at CODESA suggested, and he was still acting as if his party could keep power in its own hands. But while de Klerk was speaking inside the House, Walter Sisulu was haranguing a 'Parliament of the people' on the Cape Town Grand Parade, urging his listeners to avoid cooptation into the 'Parliament of the Boers'; and Clarence Makwetu, leader of the Pan-Africanist Congress (PAC), was telling his people in the same city that a simple democratic election to establish a constituent assembly was the only alternative to the 'monster' CODESA.[24]

Around this time, using the persuasive skills at which the National Party was particularly adept, de Klerk managed to induce enough Labour Party members to switch sides to give him control of the (Coloured) House of Representatives and therefore over the tricameral parliament. But immediately the right-wing Conservatives defeated the NP in a Transvaal by-election to announce that they were on the warpath against de Klerk's reforms.

So de Klerk changed his tactics, making the surprise announcement that in March 1992 a referendum would be held, not for all South Africans as originally stated, but for white voters only.[25] This seemed at the time to be a risky retreat into a racial political stance; but the result was a majority of more than two-thirds in favour of a continuation of the reform process, without any clear definition of what was involved. It would be hard, in the light of the result, to argue that de Klerk had been gambling; he was not that kind of politician. The result also underscored Mandela's political skill in that he persuaded his followers not to disrupt this anachronistic plan for a whites-only poll, despite the hostility it aroused among blacks. The result gave the government an opportunity to press its own arguments with greater confidence. It showed up the numerical weakness of the ebullient right wing and could only have re-assured the moderate black left wing.

But the real test was to see how these developments impacted on the activities of CODESA's five working groups. They were industrious enough, but it has been argued, notably by Steven Friedman, that their agreements were mainly in uncontested areas. Yet Working Group 1, which had a trouble-shooting assignment, found it easy to identify the sources of friction and made some progress in designing peacekeeping structures and control of the security forces.[26] Working Group 3 came up with a proposal, which was subsequently accepted, for the formation of a multiparty Transitional Executive Council (TEC) and an Independent Electoral Commission (IEC) to operate on a usefully vague 'sufficient consensus' basis. These bodies were to be given the power to ensure free political participation at national, provincial, and local levels, as well as the freedom to liaise with the black homeland governments. This group succeeded better than the others because of its procedural tightness. It passed most of its assignments over to the TEC for refinement.[27] Its work was complemented by that of Working Group 5, which concentrated on the removal of discriminatory legislation and the drafting of an electoral act.[28] The focus of Working Group 4 was on the four independent homelands (Transkei, Bophuthatswana, Venda, and Ciskei) which needed to be reincorporated into the Republic, even though, in South

African law, they were classified as totally separate entities. How their incorporation eventually happened was in fact determined by political pressures more than by constitutional decisions.

The real problem came with Working Group 2, which was deadlocked on the central issue of power. Its task was to design a shape for the new constitution: whether it should be unitary or federal; where transitional legislative power should be vested; how many legislative chambers there should be and how their members should be chosen; how the executive should be constituted; to what extent there should be separation of powers; the definition of regional (or provincial) boundaries; and – most important – by what route and by what majorities these matters would be decided.[29]

The last item proved to be the sticking point. The group recommended that a final constitution should be adopted by a national assembly while the assembly continued to act as a legislature, but it could not agree on the proportion of votes needed in the assembly for adoption of the constitution. The NP wanted a three-quarters majority; the ANC, two-thirds. At first, they compromised at 70 per cent for the adoption of the constitution and 75 per cent for the bill of rights. But the NP also wanted a 75 per cent majority for constitutional changes and equal legislative powers for the Senate. To this the ANC replied that if the constitution-making body reached a deadlock with a majority of less than 70 per cent in favour, a national referendum should be held after six months, at which a simple majority of votes would be sufficient to approve the new constitution. On these points no agreement could be reached. Both sides were trying to identify the borderline that the ANC would have to cross in an election in order to be able to push a constitution of its own devising through the assembly. Events would show that they were accurate in their calculations. But in the meantime, they were more interested in slinging mud at each other, each party accusing the other of trying to sabotage the proceedings for its own electoral advantage. The NP would have had a useful blocking mechanism with a senate of its own devising. But a statement released by the ANC's Department of Information on 13 May (the day before the government made its proposal) referred to a joint proposal by the ANC, the SACP and the Congress of South African Trade Unions (COSATU) – which had stayed together as partners of the struggle – that the constituent assembly should be a democratically elected single chamber over whose decisions no veto power should exist. Meanwhile, the eyes of party leaders were glued to the opinion polls. The NP found that it had most to gain by delay. The ANC needed a quick decision in order to carry its impatient constituency with it, especially in view of the white referendum result; and if CODESA could not produce one, there was always the avenue of popular pressure, which COSATU saw as a supplementary option in any case.[30]

Rolling Mass Action

CODESA therefore ran into the sand. The negotiations seemed to have reached deadlock, especially as Chief Mangosuthu Buthelezi had already declined to attend CODESA because it would not accord KwaZulu double representation – both for Inkatha and for the Zulu king.[31] This was of concern to the government, because the constitutional aims of Inkatha were in other respects close to those of the NP.[32] Just at this time of confrontation there occurred a ghastly massacre of ANC supporters at Boipatong, in the Vaal triangle, by 'raiders assumed to be IFP-supporting hostel residents' supposedly aided by policemen.[33] In anger, the ANC walked out of CODESA and began to prepare for a campaign of 'rolling mass action,' which was to be launched in July, leading up to a general strike on 3–4 August.[34] Following the adoption of a detailed policy document, *Ready to*

Govern, at its May congress, the ANC came up with a suggested Transition to Democracy bill in August, which short-circuited the CODESA recommendations. Among other things, it argued for the elimination of homeland boundaries.[35]

The reincorporation of the homelands into South Africa was of vital importance to the ANC, for these territories contained a large number of potential ANC voters. CODESA's Working Group 4 had run into great difficulties over this issue.[36] The ANC leaders therefore targeted three homeland governments that had held back from participation in change – Ciskei, Bophuthatswana, and KwaZulu (the last of which had never accepted 'independent' status, though this did not prevent Inkatha from asserting something not far short of it in the changed circumstances). In this spirit and against strong protests from the South African government, the ANC launched a march across the Ciskeian border to its capital, Bisho, on 7 September 1992. An opportunist change of direction by a group led by the maverick Ronnie Kasrils went past the stadium, where a rally was to be held, and through a gap in the fence towards the town itself. This provoked a violent response by Ciskeian troops, as a result of which twenty-eight marchers and one Ciskeian soldier were killed.[37]

The shooting at Bisho increased the anger but cooled the ardour of the ANC leaders. They hesitantly agreed to resume talks with the government if the government would satisfy certain conditions relating more to security matters than to constitutional ones.[38] In this turgid story of frustrating failures, we are again reminded that it had a human side, for it seems that a deep-rooted understanding between Cyril Ramaphosa, the ANC secretary general, and Roelf Meyer, the new minister of constitutional affairs, began to pay dividends.[39] Ramaphosa had taught Meyer how to catch a trout; equally to the point, both men seem to have reached the conclusion, before the collapse of CODESA, that the CODESA style had no future, that only hard bargaining between the dominant participants behind closed doors could break the deadlock – whatever effect this might have on the quality of the resultant agreement. This realization set the tone for the remainder of the constitutional negotiations right through to 1996.

A return to the table took a little while to happen, and neither side could resist continuing the slanging-match in the interim. De Klerk had offered a well-disguised eirenicon on 2 July, and Mandela eventually responded on 26 September by reducing the fourteen angry demands made right after Bisho to a mere three. This led, after tough negotiation, to a Record of Understanding between de Klerk and Mandela.[40] Then, on 1 October, Joe Slovo, the leader of the SACP, published an important recommendation, apparently at the behest of the ANC executive, for a sunset clause in the CODESA program, under which both parties would accept a transitional government of national unity, later defined as serving for a five-year period after a general election, provided the election was called soon. This could be called the second breakthrough.[41]

For those anxious for negotiations to be reopened on any workable terms, the immediate reaction was favourable. There was indeed a brief lurch towards the centre by both the PAC and the white right at the end of 1992.[42] But the members of Inkatha, who saw in it fresh evidence of ANC-NP collusion, reacted with an immediate outburst of anger and put out a lavish issue of their paper, the *Democrat*, to denounce it. Indeed, the decision drove Inkatha into an alliance (of convenience rather than anything else) with the white far right, with whom it coalesced in October as the Concerned South Africans Group (COSAG).[43]

In the first half of 1993 the white right wing showed its teeth. On 10 April, after the ANC and the NP had patched up their quarrel (in March) and reopened formal talks at the World Trade Centre,[44] a Polish immigrant, acting in collusion with an

English-speaking ex-Rhodesian, assassinated Chris Hani,[45] a young communist of great verbal skill and personal charm, who had formerly been leader of MK and had been widely regarded as the ANC's trump card for the management of its undisciplined rank and file. So popular was Hani both outside and inside the circles in which he moved that the danger of widespread public violence was immediate. However, the murder gave impetus to the speeding up of negotiations, not least as a result of Mandela's masterly appeal for moderation after the funeral.[46] Two weeks later the negotiating council at Kempton Park agreed to hold an election before the end of April 1994, and on 3 June it was set for 27 April.

This was enough for the white right-wingers. On 25 June a crowd of them, led by Eugene Terre'Blanche, leader of the Afrikaner Weerstandsbeweging (AWB),[47] ostentatiously stormed the World Trade Centre. They drove an armoured vehicle through its plate-glass doorway and occupied and trashed the chamber without opposition from the security forces outside. But this was brutal theatre rather than a coup. Moreover, the police underreaction to the violence actually paid dividends. The actors had overplayed their hand – and not for the last time. An indirect consequence was that the right-wing leadership fell into the hands of a man of strong feelings but good logistical sense and at least a touch of political realism. This was General Constand Viljoen. He had entered the chamber with the AWB; but the thuggery that followed was not his kind of political behaviour.[48]

Black right-wingers, driven by their anxiety about ANC-NP collusion and their determination to settle matters only through a fully democratic election, now began to act in rhythm with their rival white racists by indulging in terrorist acts of sly bravado under their slogan 'One settler, one bullet.' They shot up the congregation of a popular English-speaking church and a popular tavern in Cape Town, and also a golf club and restaurant in the eastern Cape, and they murdered an American exchange student, Amy Biehl, in a Cape Town black township – all reminiscent of the various shooting sprees indulged in by individual white racists from time to time, which likewise seem to have been driven by mindless fits of token genocide.[49]

While all this was going on, the bargainers at the World Trade Centre regained their composure to beaver away at a draft of the Interim Constitution and actually completed their work in time to meet the needs of the April election date. This extensive document was approved by a plenary session of the negotiating council on 17 November 1993 and enacted by Parliament on 18 December.[50] The urgency was real, for if the election date had not been adhered to, Slovo's sunset clause would have been dishonoured and the risk of violence would have been very great. As things turned out, the achievement of the constitution makers was magnified at this point by events that effectively drove the white right-wingers out of the running.

In March 1994 two of the homeland humpty-dumpties fell from power. The first was President Lucas Mangope of Bophuthatswana, after a brief but very bitter ANC-inspired revolt by public servants against his government. It would not have been overthrown if de Klerk's ministers had had their way, but it was hard to save once the AWB had decided to enter the fray, in defiance of the orders of General Viljoen (who was now leader of a newly formed Afrikaner Volksfront) and after the group indulged in a reckless shooting spree against Mangope's black opponents. Three of the AWB members were shot in cold blood by a uniformed Bophuthatswana policeman[51] after begging for mercy before the world's television cameras – and there was nothing the AWB could do to take revenge. In the end, after vain attempts by the South African government and General Viljoen to prop up Mangope, he was told to resign by Mandela and de Klerk, acting together on 12 March.[52]

The next to go was Brigadier Gqozo, ruler of Ciskei, who discreetly followed his fellow homeland leader out of power; he resigned rather than face a strike by civil servants on 22 March[53] – a significant weakening of his resistance in view of the Bisho massacre six months earlier. Firm refusals by independent homeland leaders to renounce their autonomy could not otherwise have been circumvented by the South African government by normal legal methods.

The collapse of Bophuthatswana and Ciskei left Buthelezi isolated, still in fighting mood, boycotting the constitutional talks because of the nonacceptance of his demands on behalf of the Zulu king, and by no means down.[54] In March, Inkatha impis staged an armed parade through the centre of Johannesburg in protest against the draft constitution. Sporadic violence occurred in various parts of town, leaving more than forty dead. The march itself diverged from the route agreed on with the authorities and proceeded past Shell House, the national headquarters of the ANC. Shots were fired from some directions, including the ANC building itself, and this resulted in eight more deaths. In this parallel of the Bisho march of the previous year, the roles were reversed; now it was the homeland element that had reneged on an agreement and the ANC that had to face an accusation of having overreacted in self-defence.[55]

Shell House set Buthelezi up for another bid to stop an election. He had accepted international arbitration over the king's status, but these negotiations collapsed when the parties would not agree to postpone the election.[56] One week before polling day, Buthelezi was persuaded – chiefly through the efforts of a friend, Professor Washington Okumu of Kenya – to participate in the election, on the understanding that immediately afterwards international arbitrators would again be invited to mediate over the constitutional problems. (The Government of National Unity's later failure to honour this undertaking – however remote the chance of success seemed to be – gave

Inkatha an excuse to withdraw from participating in constitution making in the hope of undermining the legitimacy of any decisions that did not comply with its own agenda.)[57]

Breakthrough to Democracy

The Independent Electoral Commission (IEC) was now faced with the task of arranging a general election for a single South Africa, where (unlike Namibia) it would not be possible for the United Nations to take control; and where, moreover, the government itself was excluded from taking part in the organization because it was seen as one party in a still incomplete peacemaking process.[58] So the IEC, under the direction of Judge Johann Kriegler, had to 'run, monitor and adjudicate the election,' which meant that the poll would be 'run by no state at all.'[59]

The transitional constitution, under whose terms the election was to be held, made provision for a two-chamber parliament holding concurrent powers with nine provincial legislatures.[60] All candidates were to be elected on party lists by proportional representation, and voters would exercise two votes at the same time – one national, the other provincial. The various parties were entitled to one seat in Parliament for every 0.25 per cent of the national vote which they obtained. For practical reasons, no voters' rolls could be drawn up in time, so all persons over eighteen, including citizens of the former independent homelands (or TBVC states), would be eligible to vote by producing identity books or simply voting cards from the Department of Home Affairs. They could vote anywhere, but provincial votes had to be cast in the relevant province if they were to count statistically in that province; this was in order to prevent the massive bussing of voters from one province to another. It was decided at the last minute, and after a good deal of disagreement among the parties, that a double ballot should be allowed so that voters could split their national and provincial votes rather than having to commit themselves to the same party at both levels. These were the main ground rules for one of the most unorthodox general elections in history – 'the first ever election which was negotiated at every crucial stage.'[61]

The Independent Electoral Commission's terms of reference were finalized only in February, when it was set the task of employing and training 300,000 workers and locating 9,000 voting stations and 900 counting stations for an expected poll ten times larger than the regular officials had ever had to handle before – though in fact these regular officials were marginalized; the role of the magistrates was restricted for the most part to commandeering premises as requested, and the role of the police was limited to maintaining order outside the polling stations and ferrying ballot boxes to the counting stations. The commission set up three directorates: one to administer the election, another to monitor it at all stages (here there was a role for foreign observers), and a third to adjudicate disputes.[62] They had to design and colour-print voting papers to carry the names of nineteen parties on the national poll (all with names, logos, and leaders' photographs) and twenty-four names on the provincial poll, not counting Inkatha's. The task of sticking Inkatha's symbols, at the last minute, onto 80 million ballot papers was achieved with fewer complications than might have been predicted.

The long waits in queues on the three days of polling (26 to 28 April) and the confusion afterwards during the counting could hardly have been avoided. Many complaints reached the IEC monitors alleging intimidation, and most of these never reached the electoral court. The level of fear and suspicion was high. All major parties were prevented by intimidation from campaigning in one region or another, and this occurred to a greater extent than it had under the previous NP regime.[63] Some of the intimidation was public and blatant, too strong for the police to control.[64] There were major problems from the nondelivery and improper handling of ballot papers and ballot boxes. The counting of votes produced insuperable problems, even at the highest IEC level, and in key instances the major parties agreed not to notice irregularities, which the IEC also was prepared to condone.[65] Yet against all this, the electoral mood was euphoric, especially among Africans, who had never voted before. Right-wing interference was minimal and ineffective, there were very few kidnappings of officials and almost no spoilt papers. In the end, the 'messy miracle' was recognized for what it was. And its result? It gave the ANC seven provinces – but fractionally less than the two-thirds majority it would have needed to rig the next constitution.[66] The NP won the Western Cape (with the help of its traditional 'black peril' tactics, which had been employed to scare Coloured voters away from the ANC camp); and Inkatha was left in menacing control of KwaZulu-Natal (where peace could hardly have endured if Inkatha had been defeated).

In terms of the transitional constitution, the country was now to be ruled by an obligatory coalition cabinet, composed of members of the parties that had gained twenty or more seats in the National Assembly, in proportion to their strength. This meant the ANC, the NP, and – ironically – Inkatha. Similar proportional arrangments had to be made in each province.

On 10 May 1994, in the amphitheatre in front of Sir Herbert Baker's Union Buildings in Pretoria, Nelson Mandela was inaugurated president, and Thabo Mbeki and F.W. de Klerk executive deputy presidents, in one of the most colourful ceremonies carried out anywhere in recent years, before a great gathering of representative foreign dignitaries. Never had South Africa seen anything like it. The speech making, especially that of the president himself, was as good as the occasion demanded. It was one of the greatest acts of reconciliation in modern times, held on a brilliant autumn day under the waving of a new, richly symbolic, and now very popular national flag to the accompaniment, at appropriate moments, of the singing of 'Die Stem van Suid Afrika' and the traditional hymn-turned-anthem in the Xhosa and Sesotho languages, 'Nkosi sikelel 'iAfrika,' 'Morena boloka sechaba sa heso' (God bless Africa).

Then came, inevitably, the ordinary light of common day. The Government of National Unity now had to face the task of building a new society out of the old bricks, with all the handicaps of an economy that had been run down under sanctions and with a school system that had as good as collapsed – and in collapsing had left a legacy of large numbers of unemployable people who had high expectations of better things. There remained, too, a residue of the immense injustices of the previous centuries in the form of demands for restitution of lost rights – to property and to work – and, not least, demands for revenge. These things survived the euphoria of May 1994. So did the public violence, which I have hardly mentioned in this chapter but which provided a continual background cacophony to the story.

The question to be answered was whether, in the face of all these tensions, the society could hold together long enough for its new political leadership to bring a new, fully legitimate political structure into being. Making peace normally comes before drafting new constitutions, but South Africa had to do both things at the same time. The next chapter will look at the peacemaking challenge. We will then turn in the third chapter to the making of South Africa's first democratic constitution and its certification by the new Constitutional Court, its promulgation over the president's signature at Sharpeville on 10 December 1996, and its coming into force at the beginning of the parliamentary session in February 1997.

2

Peacemaking

IT IS NOT AT ALL EASY to combine the two operations of making peace and drafting a constitution. Far easier is it to beat the enemy and then impose terms. In South Africa there had been no formal war, but we had had the next best thing – informal frontier conflict across the continent from Angola to Mozambique, which had been pictured as 'total onslaught' by the government in power in order to justify cross-border raids involving the use of air power, armoured vehicles, and heavy artillery, in addition to the violent suppression of resistance on the home front. A rival government in exile had wider de facto diplomatic links than the South African government, and it had access to sophisticated weaponry from the communist bloc to balance the Republic's growing arsenal of heavy armaments, which for the most part were locally produced on account of the international arms embargo. The parties in exile also had growing links with movements inside the country and had begun to sabotage state institutions by planting bombs in public places and attacking police stations in order to match the strikes of South African counterinsurgency units in foreign countries.

The existence of an informal border conflict encouraged the growth of paramilitary organizations inside as well as outside the country. A formidable crop of these had sprouted in the conditions of the 1980s, and most of them survived into the 1990s. Parts of the country were dominated by armed white units in their own symbolic liveries, notably, the pseudo-Nazi Afrikaner Weerstandsbeweging (Afrikaner Resistance Movement), the Boere Republican Army, the Oos [East] Transvaal Boerekommando, the Pretoria Kommandogroep, and the Wit Wolve (White Wolves), all of which were based mainly in the Transvaal and were recognized by the *Race Relations Survey* of 1993–4 as still being active.

Forces on the black right included the Azanian People's Liberation Army (APLA, the armed wing of the Pan-Africanist Congress) which, like the ANC's Umkhonto we Sizwe (Spear of the Nation, MK), maintained bases in the independent Transkei with that government's approval – but, unlike MK, professed to be at war with the South African government until 1994. The Azanian National Liberation Army (AZANLA) of the Black Consciousness movement was still, like APLA, involved in acts of sabotage in 1993.[1] And although Umkhonto we Sizwe had stopped fighting the government, it was carrying on its private, largely territorial feud with Inkatha and had set up self-defence units to protect its supporters in the urban townships and to resist suspected third-force violence.[2] White and black resistance movements maintained themselves with the help of firearms that found their way into South Africa chiefly from Angola and (via Swaziland) from Maputo, Mozambique, in sufficient quantities to defeat border controls. For its part, Inkatha seems to have received weapons through official Defence Force connivance.

The climate of violence which the existence of these groupings and their AK-47s brought about created space for other marginalized interest groups to arm themselves for their own reasons. Conflict between homeowners and hostel dwellers – that is, between culturally urbanized black families and rural migrant workers in town (many of them Inkatha supporters) – had broken out during the Soweto disturbances of 1976, and survived to merge with the ANC's conflict with Inkatha from the mid-1980s. Meanwhile, the weakening of government transport monopolies in the black townships, as a result of boycotts and periodic arson attacks on vehicles, led to the emergence of new taxi associations in the larger towns – speculative fleet owners who employed armed highway buccaneers to fight their battles with assault rifles for control of lucrative routes.

There was much unrest among frustrated young black adults who had been unable to complete their schooling because their schools had been destroyed (often with their own assistance) during the five-year emergency since 1985. Many of these youths had since been trained as guerrillas in exile, while others were unemployable – an element ripe for recruitment into the potentially fascist cadres that were present among black youth or into the ready-to-hand paramilitary bodies. On the other hand, if they had it in mind to obtain a graduation certificate for employment purposes, they could enter one of the universities or technikons, which no longer had race bars, either to gain learning or to use the institution as a base for coordinating group pressure of various kinds.

The party meetings at the World Trade Centre in 1991–4 took place at a time when the annual deaths from civil strife had risen from about 600–1,400 in the late 1980s to about 2,700–3,800 in the early 1990s. The mortalities in 1994 more than tripled those during the nationwide Soweto disturbances of 1976–7.[3] The issue of power was far from being resolved. The delegates knew that their task was to make peace, and most wanted to live under a single system of government; but they did not or could not separate these two processes from each other. The government was not prepared to surrender any of its authority before a general election. In fact, it even wanted to coopt ANC leaders, who had never enjoyed legal recognition, into its own cabinet. The ANC, for its part, wanted participatory control over a new interim government, including the state media, the security forces, the budget, and the election preparations.[4] It was a chicken-and-egg situation; the suppression of violence required strong government, but there could not be strong government until the parties agreed where legitimate authority was to be located.

Security Force Amalgamations

To achieve the suppression of violence, it was essential that all the military forces be drawn together, a task that was bound to be difficult, given the multiplicity of armed units and the abundance of easily accessible weapons. Compulsory military service had been discredited under the NP by its handling of recusant white conscripts. The South African Defence Force (SADF) had a reputation for dirty tricks beyond the borders, and the liberation forces were known for their attacks on soft targets, so neither would trust the other with independent power.

To marry hostile armed forces, with their variant backgrounds, structures, drill styles, and camaraderies was certainly not a simple operation, and it is important to note that the initiative for amalgamation came from the soldiers themselves and was later backed by the politicians. The Transitional Executive Council Act of 1993 provided for a force drawn from the rival armies, commanded by officers selected from the SADF, the South African Police (SAP), MK, and the Transkei and Venda security forces, but not from the security forces of the Ciskei or Bophuthatswana, which had not yet been reunited with the Republic, or from the Pan-Africanist Congress (PAC), which was still at war with the government, or from the white right-wing groups, which were hostile to change.[5]

The resultant National Peace-Keeping Force (NPKF), too hurriedly trained, failed in the first task assigned to it (to restore order in the east Rand townships in April 1994), and the SADF had to be sent in to do the job. After this, all military units were subsumed under the banner of a new South African National Defence Force (SANDF), which was under the orders of a career SADF general and a black minister of defence. Mass 'awols' over discipline and pay did not disappear overnight, though the soldiers, unlike the police, were not allowed to form their own trade union.[6] Although resistance and protest among black security forces did not completely abate, the SANDF gradually built itself up, especially after APLA members were incorporated following the PAC's decision to end its war against the government in May 1994. SADF officers, many of whom remained unapologetic for their political role in the enforcement of apartheid, contributed a necessary professionalism to the new force, which blended with MK's acceptance of a role change from that of guerrilla units to that of a national army to bring about an encouraging transition.[7]

A similar move was made to reform the South African Police[8] and to change their image, in view of the very bad reputation which these low-paid law officers had acquired in the past as administators of inhumane laws. This transformation was far from easy. Unprovoked attacks on individual policemen throughout the 1980s and early 1990s seemed to create the impression that nothing had changed.[9] But these actions were partly the result of a new determination on the part of the police to combat the increasing number of murders, rapes, housebreakings, car thefts, and hijackings, which were giving South Africa a claim to be the crime capital of the world. Since there was no police structure in the liberation movements with which the SAP could amalgamate, change had to come from a remodelling of the existing institution. This need was recognized by the SAP leadership. But although the police were anxious to break away from their image as the instruments of apartheid, they wanted to arrange the transformation themselves. By moving too slowly on this front, especially by not removing some unretreaded high-profile generals quickly enough, the SAP allowed the initiative to pass to ANC negotiators at Kempton Park, where the parties agreed to reconstitute the force as the South African Police Service (SAPS). This brought a new emphasis on community policing and the demilitarization of ranks and structures, though centralized control was substantially retained once the ANC realized how difficult it would be to maintain uniform standards if it implemented regional decentralization, as it had hoped to do. Yet the high level of corruption in the police force was not easy to eradicate overnight, and it was not known until late in 1996 how ready individual policemen would be to admit to having committed acts of brutality towards political prisoners during the apartheid era. These problems continued to undermine the SAPS's efforts at reform.[10]

Laying the Ghosts of the Past

Acts of inhumanity during the years of conflict were a big problem for both the ANC and the government. The ANC had been responsible for brutality and assassination in its detention camps in Angola, Zambia, Tanzania, and Uganda. In October 1992 it published the report of its Skweyiya Commission of Inquiry into the camps, in all of which, according to Amnesty International, there had been a 'long-standing pattern of torture, ill-treatment and execution of prisoners by the ANC's security department [which] was allowed to go unchecked for many years.' The commission noted that the ANC did not have authority in its countries of exile to bring miscreants to justice, and it blamed the governments for allowing the ANC such latitude. The ANC had in fact shown some openness, especially when Mandela appointed the independent Motsuenyane Commission in 1993, before the publication of the Skweyiya Report, but he did not release any names.[11] The Motsuenyane Report endorsed the Skweyiya Commission's central findings, severely indicted the ANC's security department for brutality, and criticized the national executive for not having kept proper control over the camps, for which the executive, not MK, was ultimately responsible.[12]

The South African government, having much more face to save, was far less candid than the ANC. There had been a great deal of brutality, mainly under laws, enacted since 1960, which had placed detainees entirely in the power of the security forces under conditions of total secrecy and without access to proper medical or legal aid. The number of political prisoners who had died in suspicious circumstances was unacceptably high.[13] The government consistently denied ANC charges that there had been, and still was, a 'third force' whose role was to eliminate targeted resistance leaders, yet there had been an escalation of unexplained political murders during the 1980s, sometimes sensationally linked to security force activity.[14] On a number of occasions the government seems to have covered its tracks with success, as in the report of the Harms Commission of 1990–1, which threw very little light on third-force activities because its inquiry appears to have been superficial and its terms of reference excluded acts performed beyond the borders.[15]

Peace Brokerage

In the interests of peace, there had to be some condonation of atrocities committed by people on both sides, but this raised some very difficult questions. How was an atrocity to be defined? At what level should blame for acts of criminal violence fall within the definition? For instance, should the blame fall on the actor alone, excluding the givers of orders and the individual or collective makers of immoral laws? And who was to do the forgiving? Should it be the victim, who keenly wanted to know whom to forgive and for what? Or should the state grant a blanket pardon, in which case how and when should this be done? Certainly, it should not be done the way President de Klerk did it – by forcing an indemnity bill through with the help of his nominated President's Council late in 1992, after it had been rejected not only by the ANC but even by the white-majority parliament. On what grounds had any government in power the right to pardon wrongful acts performed under its own authority against its opponents and expect to be taken seriously by those opponents?[16] De Klerk seems to have rushed the measure through in order to head off trouble from the militant, vulnerable, white right-wingers, and in doing so to have muddied the water for any follow-up legislation.

The new parliament, in the course of preparing a definitive constitution, examined the problem afresh in view of an agreed set of principles in the Interim Constitution, together with its bill of rights and the decision of the Constitutional Court to outlaw the death penalty.[17] But the broad issue of amnesty and compensation to victims of political violence remained in abeyance until the Government of National Unity tabled legislation to set up the Truth and Reconciliation Commission (TRC) in 1994.[18]

The unexpected flexibility of F.W. de Klerk, the moderation of Nelson Mandela, and the capacity of both men to resume contact after repeated verbal conflict gave the move towards reconciliation a rhythm which caused many to think that it was unstoppable. Events already mentioned give some credence to this line of argument. One thinks of Piet de Lange's quick recovery after Thabo Mbeki's slashing attack at the New York dinner, or the sweet reconciliation on the morning after Mandela's attack on de Klerk at the opening of CODESA, and especially his remarkable return to the negotiating table after Chris Hani's murder. But unstoppability is not a law of history. It can cease to hold true at a moment's notice. Therefore we must also take into account such positive steps as the removal of barriers to peace and the creation of conflict-resolving machinery, which were every bit as important for healing the society as the techniques for disclosing the truth about the past and which also were taken without delay.

CODESA's Working Group 1 paid much attention to the removal of obstacles to peace, though the going was heavy.[19] Meetings between the ANC and the Inkatha Freedom Party (IFP) in January 1991, and between the government and the ANC in February, led to the signing of a National Peace Accord in a rather tense atmosphere at the Carlton Hotel, Johannesburg, on 14 September.[20] But this did not prevent a 'nice document' from being drafted. CODESA took it up. The accord's most important outcome was the creation of a network of peace structures and dispute-resolution committees across the country under the supervision of a secretariat of eight, appointed by the president, with the task of resolving crises quickly as they arose. The object was to try to inculcate a culture of peacemaking throughout the country. It met with a lot of opposition, but the general election of 1994 could hardly have happened without it.[21] Its monitoring activities did much to head off trouble, especially in KwaZulu, but its cost was great in some areas, and the government wound it down in 1995.[22]

The accord was backed by the appointment of a commission of inquiry, with wide powers, under Judge Richard Goldstone.[23] By September 1993 this commission had deployed special investigation units in all the large centres, which held public inquiries and delivered open reports to the government with recommendations for action. These units looked into all major incidents[24] and also examined allegations of clandestine operations by the security forces. Goldstone's reports were initially cautious, but they grew increasingly responsive to evidence of partisan destabilization by officials in unrest situations.[25] Goldstone became correspondingly more critical of the government – for not placing security fences around township single-sex hostels (which were both sources and targets of attacks) and for not restricting the carrying of arms in public demonstrations. In May 1993 he handed de Klerk a draft bill on the regulation of public gatherings which laid responsibility on the organizers for keeping the peace.[26] Goldstone complained in December 1993 that barely half of the 149 recommendations made by his commission in the twenty-eight reports submitted had been discussed, and only 14 per cent of these had been fully implemented owing to bureaucratic inefficiency. The commission was wound up in October 1994, by which time the hit-squad activity was apparently over even if the violence was not. Its effectiveness in uncovering the hit-squad activity became clearer at the beginning of 1997, when the Truth and Reconciliation Commission publicized details from a report which General Pierre Steyn, SADF chief of staff, had given to President de Klerk early in 1994.[27]

Facing Up to Economic Realities and Popular Tensions

The situation 'out there' on the socio-economic and political fronts remained volatile. The country could as easily be pulled apart by obdurate employers unwilling to adopt new imperatives in the market or the workplace, or by rampant trade unionists with worker-oriented or political agendas, as by cadres of armed men. Burgeoning squatter movements both in the countryside and in town could lead to overreaction by property owners, causing adverse effects on food production and creating social instability.

The state of the South African economy at the dawn of the new era offered little hope of a quick recovery. The industrial system had for years underused its human potential and had created a huge skills crisis during a period of rapid population growth. The resultant generation of unemployables could be of little help at a time when the end of international sanctions required a rapid expansion of external trade – but it had to be trade in beneficiated products made by skilled workers to supplement the export of semi-processed or unprocessed minerals (of which South Africa possessed vast quantities) at internationally controlled prices. Growth was also undermined by a massive diversion of revenue to service the high-interest loans that had been raised in the sanctions era, and this led to rocketing personal taxation, a high inflation rate in comparison with the First World, and a severe shortage of capital until such time as the outside world would increase its investment – which it would not do on a sufficient scale without a clear signal that tough exchange controls were on their way out.

Although the economy was supposedly based on free-enterprise capitalism, it was as shot through with bureaucratic command structures as any in the Western world. These had sapped the competitive energies of private business to an alarming degree, and with the ending of the international trade boycott a decade after the repeal of the South African job colour bar, at a time when industrial bargaining was still a relatively new experience for both sides, labour relations entered a difficult phase. Skills that were urgently needed required a revolution in training methods, while underqualified workers wanted better wages ahead of marketable skills. Free marketeers demanded an open economy, while many workers and above all the unemployed wanted not less socialism but more.

Yet there were hopeful signs of change. Overseas investor confidence was not altogether lacking. Equally important, there was some imaginative growth in the thinking of the triple alliance of the ANC, the South African Communist Party (SACP), and the Congress of South African Trade Unions (COSATU) about economic policy. The SACP had kept up its Marxist-Leninist approach until 1990 or 1991, though some of its leaders, notably Chris Hani, leader of MK, had become cautiously conciliatory by March 1990.[28] From then on, the ideological conviction of many party members weakened, and more and more were drawn towards the ANC's moderate socialist position. Most SACP members had moved away from hard-line Marxism before their 1991 congress, influenced by communism's failure in Eastern Europe; hardly any COSATU shop stewards belonged to the SACP by that time.[29] The pull of the SACP towards a pragmatic stance was reflected in February 1992 in the joint ANC-SACP statement in favour of multiparty democracy, and above all in Joe Slovo's successful plan to break the deadlock between the ANC and the National Party with his proposal for a sunset clause to cushion the transfer of power.[30]

The ANC leadership, realizing in the stressful economic

atmosphere of the post-sanctions era that its earlier flirting with socialist ideologies might let it down, committed itself nervously to a market economy in order to re-enter world trade; but it was soon to take on board the Reconstruction and Development Programme (RDP), which had been designed by COSATU as a device to keep the triple alliance of ANC, SACP, and the unions together.[31] The RDP obtained a go-ahead from the business world, two of whose leaders were appointed to the key finance ministry in the cabinet.[32] By 1994 COSATU and the ANC were softening towards the new trade policy of Trevor Manuel and Alec Erwin, which accepted market principles as inescapable, though they reserved the right to contest the means by which the goals were to be achieved.[33] The powerful leverage exerted by strike activity since 1973 inevitably pulled COSATU in a 'workerist' direction, which could have led it into conflict with its political partners, whose concern was as much with the unemployed as with the employed. But as will be shown in the next chapter, involvement in the debates over property and lockout rights in the making of the constitution was to have the immediate effect of drawing the alliance closer together.

Another area of potential conflict was land rights. Repeal of apartheid land legislation had been initiated by laws of the de Klerk government.[34] These reforms had made provision for redress where the state had expropriated land for ideological reasons and still held it, and a land court had been set up to deal with claims to land that had passed into private hands; but they stopped short of a policy of systematic restoration. For well over a hundred years, African land rights had been seriously diminished by conquest and legislation. In some instances, Africans had moved back onto land from which they had been driven, and whites had again evicted them by force.[35]

In 1994 the Government of National Unity faced the massive task of seeing that right was done to perhaps three million people who had been dispossessed of land or forceably removed from it in the name of segregation or apartheid. The government had to find a way of doing this that would satisfy the dispossessed without driving those in possession (mainly whites) into open defiance. But whatever policy was adopted for redressing wrongs, there could be no satisfactory solution unless it adequately addressed the need to conserve the soil for posterity and ensure that the productivity of the land would be maintained or improved. Here, therefore, although a promising start had been made, there was a potentially explosive mixture of wants and considerations.

Parties in the Transition

To round off this discussion of the journey towards a culture of peace, we need to assess the impact of the political parties on the peacekeeping process.[36] Let us start, therefore, with those parties that had operated under the previous constitutions and had now accepted the necessity of sharing power.

The National Party (NP)
Founded in 1914 by General J.B.M. Hertzog, 'purified' in 1934 under D.F. Malan, and continually in power from 1948 to 1994, the NP had started out as a predominantly lower-middle-class movement concerned with protecting Afrikaner cultural rights and restoring mainly Afrikaans-speaking poor whites to prosperity in an alien English-speaking economy. It had succeeded so well that the Afrikaners had established clear cultural parity and, in taking over the state, had by the 1960s acquired a substantial share in the business sector. The party had then thrown its blanket over the interests of all white South Africans, though many non-Afrikaners resented its intrusion; it developed its apartheid doctrines out of the segregationist thinking of governments from Lord Milner's time, at the beginning of the century, as a means of rationalizing the continuance of minority white

rule. Its cohesion had begun to break down after 1966, when it started to modify the apartheid formula to meet the difficulties it could not handle, thus spawning breakaway parties under Dr Albert Hertzog (1968) and Dr Andries Treurnicht (1982), which resisted any softening of policy. The NP had admitted in 1990, through F.W. de Klerk, that it had been moving in the wrong direction: as a party, it had committed an error of judgment rather than a gigantic wrong, however much individual party members might have felt that this did not go far enough. It seems doubtful that de Klerk could have carried his party had he tried to follow the contrition route.

The party had regained some prestige by showing a willingness to share power, especially in securing a two-thirds majority among whites in favour of power sharing in the 1992 referendum. It had reversed its policy towards the mainly Afrikaans-speaking Coloured people, whom it saw as potential allies and whose relatively radical Labour Party it had already as good as co-opted. In spite of its failure to hold the line of its choice at the CODESA negotiations, it joined the Government of National Unity in 1994 in the mood of a party that still had a role to play – albeit a new-look colour-blind role – even to the point of perhaps one day being able to oust a black majority government from power. De Klerk's political campaigning made this very clear. But could the NP conceivably wish its past away to the point of baring its soul before the Truth and Reconciliation Commission? And if it could bare its soul, could it retain its following?

The Democratic Party (DP)
The DP looked for its roots to the tradition of liberal opposition that had been articulated through the Liberal Party from 1953 to 1968 and through the Progressive Party from 1959, and by taking on board survivors of the old United Party, which had been led by General Smuts during the Second World War but

had faded out in 1977. In the party's various forms, its opposition to apartheid had been fairly unequivocal, generally on the grounds of moral principle, and it had shown a preparedness to occupy the opposition benches, without the prospect of winning power, for close on half a century. Its nadir (or perhaps its zenith) in opposition had been the years 1961–74, when Helen Suzman was its only representative in Parliament. Its worst moment of crisis occurred in 1986, when its parliamentary leader, Dr F. van Zyl Slabbert, resigned from Parliament on the grounds that it was not possible to change the system by parliamentary methods. This encouraged radical opponents to label Progressives who did not follow him as being covert supporters of apartheid, despite their voting record, because of their association with business interests – though on much-debated grounds.[37]

The DP was representative mainly of the English-speaking middle class in the cities, especially in university centres. It had been the official opposition in the white parliament until the breakaway Conservative Party (CP) achieved a larger number of seats in 1987. It had been very influential in giving de Klerk his two-thirds majority in the referendum of 1992, and its leaders had played a key mediatory role in constitution making.[38] But the DP emerged from the 1994 general election, fought under proportional representation, with the right to no more than seven members in the National Assembly and three in the Senate. South Africa had moved from an elitist to a mass political system, and the DP, which resisted being labelled as an ethnic entity and had a narrow class base, lost effective leverage. With only limited funds and lacking a leader with the electoral profile of a Mandela or a de Klerk – which only regular exposure through the visual media could supply – it had been unable to reach the wider electorates or set up viable branches in marginal areas. Under these conditions, it could not prevent a slide away of white voters towards the NP and the ANC. Given its centrist, moderate, cerebral style, the DP needed to combine the role of opposition politics, in which it had learned to excel, with a capacity to disseminate enthusiasm for urgent change through the social market economy to which it professed a commitment.

The White Right-Wing Parties

By mid-1994 the white right was no longer a serious threat to South African stability, nor would it be unless there was a major collapse of the political structures, in which case its propensity for taking decisive action might well reappear.[39] The Afrikaner Weerstandsbeweging (AWB) had burned its boats by its mindless militancy and by the image it projected as a promotor of racist bigotry. But the more moderate right-wing elements retained – through Constand Viljoen's Freedom Front (FF) – a capacity to contribute to the national debate, and to be listened to with respect. The FF was angered by the declining role of the Afrikaans language in public life generally; but as with its case for a separate Afrikaner *volkstaat*, a convincing alternative deal was not easy to mount, especially in view of the claims of nine other languages alongside English and Afrikaans, all in the queue for official recognition. There remained, to a limited degree, the traditional trekking option, and some Afrikaner farmers began to make and even carry out plans to settle in Mozambique or to move even farther north. The FF appeared in its public attitudes to be resigned to change rather than proactive in support of it. But as the most acclimatized of all the cultural communities of European origin in South Africa, Afrikanerdom was in a better position than the other exotic groups to remould itself in line with the new dispensation and to stay put, despite the record of the apartheid years.

The Newcomers to Parliament

The alliance between the African National Congress and the South African Communist Party had grown out of the liberation struggle, and the grouping of these two with the Congress of South African Trade Unions (COSATU) matured during the run-up to the 1994 general election, which gave them more than 60 per cent of the vote. But COSATU, the most successful co-ordinator of black industrial unions, was only one of a number of groupings that had been involved in the internal struggle. Others included the United Democratic Front (UDF), formed in 1983,[40] which grew into the much larger, less clearly structured Mass Democratic Movement (MDM) in the next few years, and the South African National Civics Association, which had grown out of widespread opposition to the Black Local Government Act of 1983, using the rent boycott as one of its weapons. Given the earlier rift within the ANC in 1958 – in simple terms, a split between socialists and Africanists – as a result of which the minority had been expelled and had regrouped as the Pan-Africanist Congress (PAC), the danger of a rift in the dominant black alliance was obvious. Although both factions claimed loyalty to the Youth League's 1949 Programme of Action, they had remained rivals in exile and on Robben Island.

The PAC made little contribution to the national debate, its approach to the electorate being based on an appeal to African emotions rather than on coherent arguments. It demanded the transfer of all land to Africans in the name of retributive justice rather than as a contribution to the debate on resource management. Its tardy abandonment of race war as a purgative, summed up in the slogan 'One settler, one bullet,' called to mind a violent streak reminiscent of earlier times, as is suggested in two recent studies.[41] The PAC had shown signs of regrouping in the late 1980s,[42] but it lacked both the organizational skill and the funds, and it fared even worse than the DP in the general election of 1994, earning only 5 representatives in the 400-strong National Assembly. By contrast, the Azanian People's Organization (AZAPO) underpinned its loyalty to Black Consciousness with a socialist creed and tried to work towards a 'democratic antiracist workers' republic of Azania. But its brand of radicalism bore little resemblance to that of Steve Biko; it remained militant in outlook and, rather like Oswald Pirow's New Order group in the 1940s, lost much influence through not taking part in negotiations during the transition period.[43]

The problem of reconciling the expectations of political exiles with those of the oppressed who had stayed at home was most clearly evident in the relationship between the ANC and Buthelezi's Inkatha Freedom Party, the wildest card in the negotiating pack. In 1975 Buthelezi had revived Inkatha, a Zulu cultural movement of the 1920s, and turned it into a political pressure group that gained total control of the KwaZulu homeland legislature, basing its mystique on the wearing of tribal dress and the display of 'cultural weapons' (clubs, spears, and shields) on ceremonial occasions, and on the traditions of the Zulu monarchy, of which Buthelezi claimed, as head of his clan, to be the hereditary chief minister.[44] He had blocked NP attempts to force homeland independence on KwaZulu in the 1970s and had tried to bring the other homeland leaders into line. Similarly, he had fought hard against the exclusion of Africans in P.W. Botha's constitution. He backed a free-enterprise economy, a move that pleased Natal businessmen, many of whom endorsed the proposal of a commission named after him in 1986 to federate Natal and KwaZulu. However, this was turned down by the NP government; in any case, radical Natal Africans condemned Inkatha's elitist origins. But when in 1982 Buthelezi successfully blocked an attempt by the NP government to cede northern KwaZulu to Swaziland, a foreign state, by taking his case to the appeal court, he projected himself as a force to be reckoned with – as the ANC was finding to its cost.

Yet Buthelezi's standing in black politics had been declining ever since 1979, when he and the ANC leaders in exile had fallen out. Two previous Zulu leaders, John Dube and Albert Luthuli, had been ANC presidents, and Inkatha incorporated

ANC colours in its flag. But popular opposition to Botha's 1983 constitution, which had led up to the formation of the Mass Democratic Movement (which was secretly allied to the ANC) upset the political balance in Natal. Some Natal chiefs who belonged to a newly formed traditional leaders' association to fight apartheid, CONTRALESA, supported the MDM. Then, just when Buthelezi most needed to prove his credentials as an opponent of apartheid, the NP government began to support him as a counterweight to the ANC, giving him plenty of exposure on public television – with predictably damaging results: open conflict between the ANC and Inkatha broke out in Natal and Zululand.[45] To make matters worse, the image of the KwaZulu police was tarnished by evidence of its complicity in third-force activities.[46] Inkatha thus acquired the reputation of being a disruptive force in the move towards national unity on account of the manipulative skills of its temperamental leader, in spite of the moderation of his economic outlook.

Violence in Natal and KwaZulu did not abate after the meetings between Buthelezi and Mandela in early 1991.[47] When the ANC and de Klerk's government made their peace after the failure of the ANC's Bisho *coup d'état*, Inkatha tried to undermine the 'Record of Understanding' between de Klerk and Mandela.[48] Buthelezi wanted to ensure that there would not be a general election to choose a parliament with constitution-making powers; the constitution had to be drawn up first. Hence his refusal to attend the World Trade Centre negotiations of June 1993 and his insistence on outside arbitration to determine the status of the Zulu monarch, and – just before the general election – the demonstration outside the ANC headquarters in Johannesburg in March 1994, which turned to violence.[49]

In the light of all this, Buthelezi's last-minute decision to take part in the April general election – induced by timely private approaches[50] – posed more questions than it answered; and when Inkatha gained sufficient votes to give Buthelezi a cabinet seat in the Government of National Unity, the problems were compounded rather than reduced. Inkatha's stance, more than any other single factor, served to emphasize the indivisibility of peacemaking and constitution building. For this reason, it is necessary to look at the subject in detail, which we shall do in the next chapter.

3 〜

Constitution Making

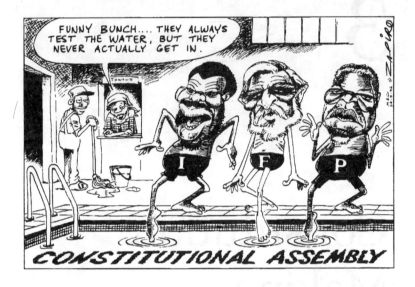

Mangosuthu Buthelezi, Walter Felgate, and Frank Mdlalose, leaders of the Inkatha Freedom Party, fought hard for a semi-independent KwaZulu-Natal. They participated in the 1994 elections but refused to take part in the Constitutional Assembly on the grounds that the Government of National Unity had reneged on a promise to allow international arbitration of their differences. (Cartoon by Zapiro. *Mail and Guardian*, 26 September 1995)

THE FORMATION OF THE UNION OF SOUTH AFRICA in 1909–10 was a coming together of four colonies (two of them previously Boer republics) on terms which they had agreed among themselves. The Westminster parliament enacted as the South Africa Act only those provisions which the colonies' dominant parties and official oppositions had proposed and tested in their separate legislatures (and, in Natal, also with a voters' referendum).

The thirty parliamentarians belonging to government and opposition parties who met round the table to draft a constitution for the Union of South Africa were all white. It was a meeting of the winners and losers of the Anglo–Boer War. The composition of this group was for long unquestioned, even though there was a much stronger expression of black opposition to the convention than historians recognized for a good fifty years.[1]

Why Britain was prepared to allow the adoption of a whites-only constitution has been fully debated, and several understandable explanations have been offered.[2] What people did not properly understand was the difficulty of actually changing an entrenched power balance once it had taken shape. The South Africa Act gave a white minority and an Afrikaner majority within that minority an incentive never to let go of their hold over the country – and much to fear should they do so. Their retention of power in 1909 enabled whites to indulge in a segregationist pipe dream, which was maintained as the central thrust of public policy for ninety years, dating from the appointment of Lord Milner's intercolonial Native Affairs Commission in 1903. This made it convenient and safe to direct their electioneering towards the relatively risk-free issue of relations between the Union and the Commonwealth – an issue that kept alive the resentment in the northern Afrikaner communities over the loss of independence in 1902. Republican sentiment lay behind General Hertzog's anti-imperial gyrations between 1912 and 1926, though he was able to retreat graceful-ly, via the Statute of Westminster, into a dream world of pseudo-independence. In this frame of mind he awoke with a start on the outbreak of war against Germany in 1939, having believed that, with dominion status, the option of neutrality would be automatic and a contrary vote unthinkable. Not until 1960, when South Africa became a republic outside the Com-monwealth, did the republican issue die down.

The first republican constitution, adopted in 1960, replaced the queen and the governor general with a dual-purpose state president in top hat and sash, and nominally broke the formal imperial link, though it preserved most of the positive ties that had made the connection worth having, especially in the areas of cultural contacts and trade.[3] Africans and Coloured people, who had been given token, indirect representation in the Cape under the constitution of 1909, were deprived of this by laws made between 1936 and 1968, which left control of Parliament entirely in white hands.[4] Thus was realized the principle that other races should have political representation only in separate advisory councils or homeland governments. Even this sur-vived its realization for barely a decade. After its separate representative council for Coloured people had failed, the Vorster government in 1977 dreamed up a constitution with three entirely separate parliaments, on the curious argument that if these parliaments were technically separate there would be no 'power sharing.' When, after Vorster's fall from power, P.W. Botha gazetted a bill in 1979 for a single parliament with three houses (one for whites, one for Coloured people, and one for Indians – but none for Africans, be it noted), this semantic adjustment caused a right-wing breakaway in protest against even so mild a form of power sharing.[5]

P.W. Botha's constitution of 1983, now headed by an execu-tive rather than a formal president, was the first timid attempt at power sharing, and it obtained a two-thirds majority in a white referendum.[6] It nevertheless ran into a massive political storm, thus precipitating greater changes, which some of its backers as well as its opponents had probably foreseen and hoped for. So when negotiations began during the late 1980s between the ANC and Mandela on the one hand, and the Botha and de Klerk governments on the other, it seemed clear that the end of a road had been reached. There had to be either a stiffening of authoritarian control, with all the hazards that this would entail for a demoralized and run-down society, or a real break with the past. The African National Congress (ANC) and the other black liberation movements had no doubt that a total break was required – hence their escalation of the conflict during P.W. Botha's period of office; but the ANC itself came to see that it did not have the muscle, after years of guerrilla conflict, to force the change. Nor did it have the kinds of insight needed to turn the economy around. To its credit, it came to admit this. All of which helps to explain why, despite the distance that separated the government from the ANC leadership, de Klerk and Mandela found it necessary to hang together, tangled in a web which they were powerless to unravel.

Creating the Machinery for Change

Self-governing states can give themselves a new constitution by causing it to grow out of an existing legal system. This the National Party (NP) tried to do at the Convention for a Democratic South Africa (CODESA) and afterwards. The NP argued that it was the holder of legal power and that a break in legal continuity would invite anarchy. The ANC, on the other hand, took its stand on the very different concept of legitimacy, asking the question 'Who has the moral right to power?' rather than 'Who has got power by right?' It feared that the Nationalists would use their existing control of power and patronage to manipulate a new constitution to their own advantage, just as the Nationalists feared that the ANC would create anarchy and in doing so would send the political system spinning out of control. The Democratic Party (DP) looked for 'a marriage of legitimacy and legality that will restore authority and order.' It was this that the negotiators at Kempton Park devised, through a constitutional (as opposed to a constituent) assembly, thus ensuring that South Africa went through a transitional as opposed to a revolutionary process.

The route taken was to set up an ad hoc semi-official administrative body to work with, watch, and, in key areas, control the existing government with the willing support of the government itself.[7] Arrangements to avoid a power vacuum between the passage of the constitution and the election that had to follow were provided for in chapter 15 of the Interim Constitution. This confirmed the legality of all existing laws[8] and ensured continuity from the existing parliament to the next[9] and from the existing presidency and cabinet to the new ones,[10] with similar provisions for the public service,[11] financial controls,[12] the judicial system,[13] local government,[14] and educational structures.[15]

The negotiating council, consisting of the parties represented at Kempton Park, set up a strong technical committee to devise the machinery to bring in a new constitution. It included several constitutional lawyers, some of whom had recently played a similar role in the making of the Namibian constitution.[16] This technical committee, assisted by its own subcouncils to deal with problem areas, gave advice on how to resolve differences, with special regard to the structure of the presidency, the membership and decision-making procedures of the cabinet, the powers of the Senate, the rights of parties in relation to elected members, the Constitutional Court, and the place of traditional rulers.[17]

To facilitate change while preserving the legalities, CODESA had proposed that the cabinet should co-opt individuals who until then had been prevented by race from participating in government, but this proposal died with CODESA. The new negotiating council decided in 1993 to set up an altogether new Transitional Executive Council (TEC), which would have collateral authority with the cabinet in one area alone: preparing the ground for a general election. Its legality rested on, and was in effect sustained by, a mutual agreement between the two dominant parties in the negotiating council, which won the reluctant support of the other parties by 'sufficient consensus' on 7 August 1993. Bophuthatswana and Ciskei, together with the Conservative Party (CP) and the Inkatha Freedom Party (IFP), opposed it. The Pan-Africanist Congress (PAC) and Afrikaner Volksunie reserved their positions. But the major parties and the DP carried it through. Its status was confirmed by legislation on 23 September, was promulgated in December to synchronize with the adoption of the Interim Constitution, and lapsed with the appointment of the first Government of National Unity the following May.

The Transitional Executive Council's actual powers were strictly limited. It could intervene if the government used its advantage to tilt the election, and an appeal against its decisions could be made to a special electoral court provided for in the Independent Electoral Commission Act; but it found that consultation rather than assertiveness was the best way to achieve its purposes.[18] Its existence gave cover for the negotiators at Kempton Park to hasten the drafting of the Interim Constitution, which was completed on 17 November 1993, in time for Parliament to enact it on 18 December.

One of the greatest fears of the ANC's opponents was that it would try to push through a constitution to its own liking by simple weight of numbers, but this it did not do. It accepted a two-stage approach, with the backing of the DP, against an assurance that a revised constitution would be drawn up and sanctioned by a fully representative parliament sitting as a constitutional assembly after a general election. But although the Interim Constitution was transitional, its significance was certainly not ephemeral. There were two reasons for this. First, the thinking and bargaining that took place during the debates of the negotiating council were likely to leave a strong imprint on the succeeding draft. Second, Parliament entrenched a series of thirty-four principles in the constitution, which were explicitly affirmed by the ANC, the party most likely to be in a position to overturn them.[19] The Constitutional Assembly was required to complete its work within two years, in preparation for a general election to be held under it on 30 April 1999.[20]

The Rules behind the Rules

The constitutional principles required the establishment of a single nonracial, nonsexist, democratic sovereign state, adhering to a code of fundamental rights under an entrenched constitution that ensured equal protection for all and entrenched the equalization of opportunity. The governmental structure was to be based on a three-tier system with separation of powers and with the rule of law under the protection of an independent judiciary. It was to be an open, representative multiparty democracy with regular elections, protection for minority parties, universal adult suffrage, a common voters' roll, and 'in general' proportional representation. Government was to be accountable. Proper law-making procedures were to be observed. There was to be nondiscriminatory freedom of association, and there was to be 'recognition and protection' for traditional leadership under indigenous law. Provincial rights, which had to include acceptable boundaries and sufficient financial muscle (under the supervision of a central financial and fiscal commission) were to be guaranteed, and changes were to be dependent on the consent of provincial legislatures. The legislative powers of the national and provincial assemblies were to be made 'concurrent,' subject to rational requirements; though 'for the maintenance of essential national standards' and services, and in order to sustain a common economic policy, along with national security and foreign relations, the central government was granted the power to take initiatives in these areas as long as it did not invade the 'geographical, functional or institutional integrity of the provinces.' Employers' and workers' associations were to be guaranteed, along with fair labour practices, and there was to be provision for an impeccable reserve bank and a pensionable public service that would be 'representative of the [whole] South African community'; as well, there was provision for disciplined and obedient security forces and for a national executive and legislature that was to hold office responsibly until the scheduled election date.

It would prove hard to resolve all difficulties: to create a bill of rights that would protect all individuals while allowing traditional rulers their customary use of arbitrary power; to concede territorial exclusiveness to cultural communities that could not be territorially defined; or to achieve exact boundaries between different levels of government when the clear intention was to give full scope to all. But they were well-defined provisions, wide-ranging in coverage, explicit as to general intent, intelligently flexible in their language, and, above all, binding.

The most divisive issues in the negotiating council may conveniently be considered under five headings: (A) Fundamental rights; (B) relationships between the executive and the legislature, linked to some kind of adherence to a separation of powers; (C) the relationship between the national and provincial authorities, in the light of federal hopes, financial problems, and Afrikaner and traditionalist claims to special political treatment; (D) local government; (E) the courts. In the following pages, for the sake of maintaining a sense of direction, I shall look at each of these areas separately, examining how they were handled in the debates over both the Interim Constitution and the New

Text,[21] and singling out issues of special relevance in view of
the experiences of South Africans in the immediate past.

A. Fundamental Rights

This was a matter to which the ANC and the DP attached special
importance and which the NP now saw fit to treat seriously. So
thoroughly had ethnic-group rights been substituted for individual rights in the apartheid era, and so frequently had the
common-law rights of individuals been ignored by Parliament
and some courts that there was, understandably, a strong com-
pulsion after the de Klerk–Mandela breakthrough to focus on
the liberty of the subject in all possible ways. The NP government had seen this coming, and its fear of losing power had
already led it to ask the statutory law commission to investigate
the problem. The commission's two reports[22] clearly laid down
that 'cultural, religious and linguistic values should *not* be
protected as group rights' because a group was not seen as a
legal *persona*. It went on to argue, however, that 'political group
rights, that is to say, the question of the nature, composition
and subdivisions of the legislature, should be protected in the
constitution itself, subject to the principle of equality.'[23]

This distinction enabled the NP to go along with the ANC and
the DP in accepting that group rights stood condemned as a
residue of the apartheid system; but the NP was loath to reject
the protection of political groups in the constitution itself. In the
ensuing negotiations, it therefore paid a lot of attention to the
safeguarding of white minority interests, as can be seen from its
proposals for a rotating three-headed presidency, a blocking
senate, and the shielding of provincial rights against central
interference, all of which created the possibility of some
minority-party control.[24]

But the negotiating council ignored group rights and concerned itself almost entirely with those of the individual.

Debate centred on the question of whether the bill should be limited to the protection of the individual against the state or extended to include 'horizontal' rights between persons; and whether it should include or omit the protection of a wider range of rights in the cultural, economic, health, and environmental fields. The negotiators, accepting that the Constitutional Assembly would later be able to modify their conclusions, opted for the inclusive approach, which was later accepted by the Constitutional Assembly itself.[25] On these issues the Constitutional Court, which was called on to handle objections to the New Text in September 1996, also took a broad view, refusing to invalidate horizontal rights *qua se* or to throw out environmental rights on the dubious ground that they were not justiciable.[26]

The constitution drawn up by the negotiating council provided a broadly inclusive list of the normal 'first generation' rights safeguarding the liberty of the subject, over most of which there was little controversy. Freedom of speech and of political expression and association caused no problems – save at the Constitutional Assembly stage, when the DP successfully amended an ANC proposal to deny protection to hate speech linked to warmongering or incitement of imminent violence, or based on 'race, ethnicity, gender or religion' unless it constituted 'incitement to cause harm.'[27]

The Interim Constitution contained a lengthy section (s. 35) on the rights of detained and arrested persons, which had grown considerably by the adoption of the New Text (s. 37) as the committee sought to sweep away the methods developed by the security forces under NP rule for annihilating resistance by political prisoners (and in many cases the prisoners themselves) without negating the capacity to legislate for a state of emergency short of proclaiming martial law. The Constitutional Assembly now tightened parliamentary monitoring of executive action and restored common law rights to detained persons across a broad front.[28]

An issue that attracted much attention was the right to life. This necessarily brought up the problem of the death penalty, which had been abolished with specific reference to this principle in the first judgment of the Constitutional Court in June 1995, a decision confirmed by the Constitutional Assembly in 1996 despite a considerable popular backlash, especially in the NP (which opted for its restoration) and among members of the ANC as well, as a result of revelations made in evidence to the Truth and Reconciliation Commission.[29]

Disagreement was predictably wide on the germane question of abortion, and the Constitutional Court ruled that the right to 'all universally accepted fundamental rights' as guaranteed in constitutional principle 2 left the formulation of such rights in the hands of the Constitutional Assembly.[30] To have decided otherwise would have been for the court to act as a moral adjudicator as distinct from a court of law, and this it was not required to do.

Children's rights were given explicit protection (s. 28) in view of the worldwide publicity given to child abuse. The rights of women, referred to in constitutional principle 1 and in the equality clauses of the Interim Constitution and the New Text, were to be cared for through the appointment of a gender commission (s. 187), whose members were nominated in November 1996.

Some rights with economic implications, such as freedom from forced labour and freedom of movement, created no problem, especially in the light of the colour bar and pass law experience. Much behind-the-scenes negotiating took place between the parties, involving business and COSATU as well, before major differences came into the open. The Interim Constitution balanced the workers' right to strike with that of employers to impose a lockout,[31] and the latter right was equally recognized in the Labour Relations Act of 1995 (promulgated only in November 1996). Before the adoption of the New Text on 8 May 1996, COSATU, backed by the ANC and not opposed by the NP, fought a public campaign to have lockout rights removed from the constitution. The Constitutional Assembly then sought a compromise by inserting a new section 241, which gave protection to the Labour Relations Act and, indirectly, to its lockout provision; but this was thrown out by the Constitutional Court as 'impermissibly shielding' an ordinary law from constitutional review. The Constitutional Court also argued that the strike and the lockout could not be seen as direct counterbalancing mechanisms on the ground that, while the collective withholding of labour was the only substantial weapon that labour could use, employers had the power to dismiss workers, take on scab labour, and alter terms of employment as well.[32]

Property rights were not directly referred to in the constitutional principles, though the Interim Constitution had guaranteed 'the right to acquire and hold rights in property' as well as ensuring proper legal procedures and compensation for any that was expropriated (s. 28). On the former issue, the ANC had itself departed from its earlier acceptance of the principle of property rights, and its stance had been fortified by the proceedings at a parliamentary workshop at the end of 1995, where exclusion of the right to property had been strongly urged, notably by speakers from the Witswatersrand University law school, but had been contested with equal strength by farming and other propertied interests.[33] For the sake of defusing the conflict, the New Text (s. 25) made no mention of the right to property; but as a result of the insistence of NP and DP spokespeople, the grounds for and procedures regarding expropriation were brought under the limitations clause (s. 36), thereby requiring explicit guarantees to owners, under a law of general application, before expropriation could take place.[34]

A debate was bound to develop on cultural and language rights over the interpretation of constitutional principle 11, which stated, 'The diversity of language and culture shall be acknowledged and protected, and conditions for their promotion shall be encouraged.'[35] Although English was made the language of record for practical purposes (even Afrikaans being demoted for this reason), the legislators announced in section 6 of the New Text that the official languages were to be Sepedi, Sesotho, Setswana, siSwati, Tshivenda, Xitsonga, Afrikaans, English, isiNdebele, isiXhosa, and isiZulu. Flexibility was to be used at all levels of government according to their different regional needs, provided that at least two official languages were used; and the Pan–South African Language Board was to promote also the Khoi, Nama, San, and sign languages, and to ensure respect for all other languages spoken by minorities or used in South Africa for religious purposes. For the first time, provision was made for simultaneous translation in Parliament. Whereas, previously, separate English and Afrikaans editions of Hansard had been published, these were to be replaced by a single Hansard in which all speeches in Afrikaans would be translated into English (with asterisks to indicate translations), and those made in the African languages would be given in the vernacular, followed by bracketed translations.

The Constitutional Assembly decided that 'everyone has the right to receive education in the official language or languages of their choice in public educational institutions where that education is reasonably practicable' and that 'the state must consider all reasonable educational alternatives, including single-medium institutions' to promote this end. This formulation had special relevance to schools in areas where Afrikaans had been the sole medium and where – as at Potgietersrus in the Northern Province – there had been strong parental resistance to the admission of black pupils for the first time. In view of the determined effort of the government to abolish racially segregated education and to move rapidly towards the provision of equitable schooling for children of all races, its acceptance of single-medium schooling where circumstances made this appropriate on economic grounds was conditional on these schools not being racially exclusive.[36]

B. *The Executive and the Legislature*

The second divisive issue was the relationship between the executive and the legislature. If the intentions of the 1983 constitution had prevailed, the fragmented South African state that had been entrenched under the tricameral parliamentary system could not have been reunited without separate decisions being made by the four independent homelands to surrender the independence that had been conferred on them. But Transkei was willing to bargain for favourable terms; Bophuthatswana succumbed after its painful revolution; Ciskei buckled in the heat generated by Bophuthatswana's collapse; and Venda asked for reincorporation from sheer lack of resources to survive.[37] Thus, except for the fact that the concept was challenged by KwaZulu, developments before the 1994 election had in effect re-created a single South African state.

As regards the structure of government, constitutional principle 6 laid down that 'there shall be a separation of powers between the legislature, executive and judiciary, with appropriate checks and balances to ensure accountability, responsiveness and openness.' What emerged was a form of mixed government. The Interim Constitution provided for a president elected by the National Assembly and for vice-presidents representing parties that had twenty seats in that body. The ANC chose Thabo Mbeki; the NP, F.W. de Klerk. The president was to allocate cabinet posts to parties, and the parties were to fill them – an arrangement described as a 'masterpiece of political compromise' between parliamentary and presidential systems of responsible government, tailor-made for a Government of National Unity that was to hold office for five years.[38] As Colin Eglin pointed out, it was a constitution that 'does not make for the excessive concentration of powers.'[39] But in a cabinet based on proportionality rather than consensus, the convention of collective responsibility proved difficult to sustain. In the text adopted in 1996, even before the NP's decision to leave the GNU, the president was to nominate a single vice-president (Mbeki being his choice) and to fill all cabinet posts at his discretion.

One aim of the legislators was to ensure that the parliament remained answerable to the electorate – hence the encouragement of public access to it, in both its legislative and constituent capacities, and participation through parliamentary committees, and the empowerment of the assembly itself to initiate legislation through those committees, independent of the cabinet.[40] On the other hand, some provisions that began in the Interim Constitution and survived into the New Text tended to overstress the role of political parties. Elections to the much-enlarged National Assembly of 400 members were still to be based on simple proportional representation in place of the previous single-member delimitation, at least until the 1999 election and perhaps thereafter. Each province was treated as a single constituency, for which the various parties drew up their own lists of candidates. An early proposal by the DP to combine proportional representation with the constituency principle was rejected as being too complex for an untrained electorate. More controversially, the drafters ruled out a member's right to cross the floor, requiring such a member instead to resign and give way to the next candidate on the party's list. Although proportional representation was difficult to combine with by-elections, this 'anti-defection clause' came in for criticism because it protected members from being answerable to a specific electorate.[41] Even if parties could allocate constituencies to individual MPs (as the ANC did with its 251 National Assembly members and 60 senators), this did not make them responsible to those voters. The anti-defection clause survived into the New Text, but there was continuing pressure, especially from the DP, for the restoration of a constituency system in some form.

C. Federal Decentralization: Powers for Provinces, but an Afrikaner Volkstaat and Power for Traditional Leaders Placed on Hold

The ghost of federalism had stalked South African political thinking since the 1850s – frequently proposed but never previously accepted. There had been a particularly vociferous debate about it in 1907–9.[42] On that occasion, a great deal of emphasis had been laid on its financial implications, for it was seen as a very expensive form of government, largely on the basis of incomplete information received from Canada and Australia.[43] It does not seem as if negative financial arguments weighed as heavily on the minds of the Constitutional Assembly in 1994–6. Federalism necessarily implied an increase in the cost of government and the possibility of the taxpayer being mulcted from several sources. For this reason, the DP proposed a statutory financial and fiscal commission to ensure an equitable share of national revenue between provinces, along with central supervision of the taxes imposed and loans raised by the provincial governments. This suggestion found its way through into the New Text as a device for ensuring an equitable division of revenue at all levels of government from a central revenue fund.[44]

The approach in the 1990s differed from that of earlier years in that although the ANC in particular favoured centralized government in order to promote a strong national policy (just as General Smuts had argued in 1909), federalism was supported by the DP as a necessary hedge against centralized despotism, and by the NP (whose traditional attitude had been strongly antifederal) because it feared a strong government in hands other than its own, especially in the hands of the ANC.

The ANC countered with 'regionalism' – the creation of regional authorities that would have administrative but no law-making powers. Although the ANC looked hard at federalism once it saw the Senate as a possible vehicle for provincial representation, it was very unwilling to weaken the centre (even to the point of doubting the value of a Senate), because centrifugal tendencies could easily get out of hand.[45] The ANC was worried about the Afrikaner right wing's continuing demand for a *volkstaat*, which was matched by the traditional leaders' increasing insistence on the restoration of their historic political powers, and above all by Inkatha's persistent propagation of looser, confederal ideas.

The word 'federalism' did not appear in the constitutional principles, perhaps because of the ANC's reservations; but the substance of a federal constitution was implied in at least ten of the principles, above all in principle 21, which stated explicitly that either 'exclusive' or 'concurrent' powers should be granted to the provinces with respect to planning, development, and services, and to the 'specific socio-economic and cultural needs' and 'general well-being' of the inhabitants.

With the termination of the tricameral parliament and the abolition of the President's Council (the nominated body which had been used to push F.W. de Klerk's controversial indemnity bill into law) in July 1993,[46] space was provided in the Interim Constitution for the restoration of an upper house. The result was a senate of ninety members, composed of ten senators for each of nine new provinces. The New Text of 1996 converted this body into the National Council of Provinces (NCOP), an option first placed before the Constitutional Assembly in October 1995, with the intention of strengthening provincial power at the expense of the central power. Its decisions were to be determined by a majority of the bloc votes of the provincial delegations, which were to be cast by each delegation's head, who normally would be the provincial premier.[47]

The NCOP was granted law-making powers (including the right to initiate legislation) over nearly fifty specific areas relating to provincial and local government, together with the right to enter into dispute with the National Assembly and, failing agreement between the houses, to appeal to a mediation committee. This step could lead either to the lapse of the bill or to its passage by a special majority of the National Assembly.

There remains the question of the relative legislative competence of the central parliament and the provincial legislatures. The Interim Constitution referred to 'functional legislative areas' of concurrent national and provincial competence, and exclusive provincial competence.[48] 'Concurrency' meant that residual powers were vested in the central legislature 'only to the extent' that this was required by the clear need to establish uniformity throughout the land in such fields as external relations, the economy, and other areas of general policy. Such an arrangement held great possibilities for litigation, as the negotiators were well aware – hence the New Text's explicit lists of functional areas for both concurrent and exclusive provincial responsibilities.[49]

The tendency of the German model on which the Interim Constitution draft was based was to leave residual authority clearly with the central legislature in the event of conflict of laws. Appeals to the Constitutional Court in 1996 included the assertion that the New Text had actually weakened the power of the provinces *vis-à-vis* that of the central legislature. The key issue here was the bloc-voting procedure laid down for the NCOP,[50] a procedure likely to reinforce the influence of the ANC through its control over the majority of provinces and its majority control in the National Assembly. The Constitutional Court devoted much of its time to the consideration of this objection and withheld its endorsement of the New Text partly on this ground, causing the Constitutional Assembly to readjust the New Text, to the slight advantage of provincial rights.[51]

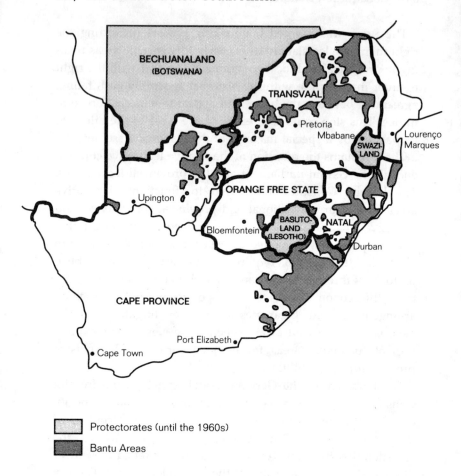

Protectorates (until the 1960s)

Bantu Areas

MAP 1 **Provincial borders**

(a) The four provinces – Cape Province, Orange Free State, Transvaal, and Natal – (1910 to 1994) and the Bantu homelands of the Old South Africa (1970s to 1994). (Adapted from the Report of the Tomlinson Commission, 1955)

(b) The nine provinces of the New South Africa, laid down in 1994 and confirmed in the new constitution of 1996.

MAP 2 **Variant versions of a possible Afrikaner** *volkstaat*
(a) The 'chopping block for negotiations' first drawn by the
    Afrikaner Volksfront (predecessor of Constand Viljoen's
    Freedom Front). This can be contrasted with a much smaller
    area, covering the southeastern Transvaal, proposed by the
    breakaway Afrikaner Volksunie and roughly delineated here by
    a broken line. (*Weekly Mail*, 9–15 July 1993)

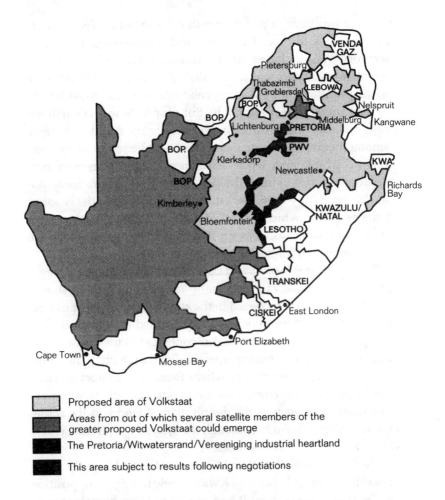

Proposed area of Volkstaat

Areas from out of which several satellite members of the greater proposed Volkstaat could emerge

The Pretoria/Witwatersrand/Vereeniging industrial heartland

This area subject to results following negotiations

(b) The Conservative Party's ideal Boerevolksrepubliek of March 1994, based mainly on the old Boer republics, but recognizing the existence of the vanishing homelands. In 1995 the *volkstaat* council, formed in response to the Constitutional Assembly's invitation to keep the topic on the agenda, used much of the Afrikaner Volksfront's outline and proposed autonomy for several more regions where Afrikaners were relatively numerous. (*Argus*, 2/3 April 1994 and 27/28 May 1995)

There was never a real chance that the Freedom Front would be granted a territorial *volkstaat*, and no provision for such a territory was included in the constitutional principles. The negotiators made room for a *volkstaat* council, which reported to the president on 25 May 1995 and later made representations to the Constitutional Assembly. But despite Mandela's willingness to hear them through, the *volkstaters* could not agree among themselves where their state might be set up, since there was no sizable area where Afrikaners could claim numerical predominance.[52] During the debate in the Constitutional Assembly on 8 May 1996, General Viljoen referred to the *volkstaat* issue as one on which 'we could not in the time available reach sufficient consensus,' though it remained 'an ideal which we will continue to pursue.'[53]

The traditional leaders and customary law presented a bigger problem. Principle 13 stated that traditional leadership should be recognized and protected in the constitution and that indigenous law should be recognized and applied by the courts, but 'subject to the fundamental rights contained in the Constitution and to legislation dealing specifically therewith.' This gave customary rights no chance where there was conflict of laws. But in practice, the chiefs exercised wide discretionary powers in crucial areas such as the distribution of land and the settlement of disputes. Archaic though the system was, it was widely accepted in rural communities.

The Congress of Traditional Leaders of South Africa (CONTRA-LESA) had come into being in KwaNdebele in 1987, in opposition to the homeland system. It had spread to other homelands, including KwaZulu, where it developed an ambivalent relationship with Inkatha.[54] A Council of Traditional Leaders was provided for in the Interim Constitution (s. 184), but the sensitiveness of the issue became apparent in May 1995, when traditional leaders were invited to the Constitutional Assembly to present their cases.[55] The Natal delegation was divided, some backing

Buthelezi, others the ANC.[56] The relevant working committee of the Constitutional Assembly handled the matter cautiously, especially since Buthelezi insisted that the chiefs' salaries should be paid by the provincial rather than the central government. The New Text left the definition of their role to national or provincial legislation. A further CONTRALESA delegation to the management committee of the Constitutional Assembly on 18 April 1996 had no greater success, and revised legislation in 1997 turned their council into a representative body of provincial chiefs with advisory powers only and no overlapping membership with Parliament or the provincial legislatures.[57]

Inkatha presented its case as the test issue for its return to the Constitutional Assembly after the Constitutional Court had considered the New Text. Inkatha's demand was that traditional leaders should have the right to establish municipalities in rural areas. The court had not gone as far as this, recommending only that chiefs of communities that observed indigenous law and resided on land within the area of transitional rural or representative councils could be *ex officio* members of such councils until 30 April 1999 or if so empowered by legislation.[58] The Constitutional Assembly was very concerned about the absence of professional qualifications required for traditional leaders and the nondemocratic nature of their authority, which could bring it into conflict with the Bill of Rights, especially with regard to the rights of African women – on whose behalf, they were clear, the Bill of Rights should have precedence.

Another consideration was the linkage made by Inkatha, in particular, between the traditional structures in the 'Kingdom of KwaZulu' and KwaZulu's demand for a semi-independent status within the Republic. It seems unlikely that Inkatha had secessionist intentions, but the issue had become politically sensitive because of the centrifugal trend that might be set off if KwaZulu's demands – highlighted by the determination of the KwaZulu legislature to define its relationship to the

Republic in a provincial constitution of its own – were given too much encouragement.[59]

D. Local Government

This, the fourth issue singled out for discussion, was seen by the negotiating council as the lowest rung of a streamlined three-tier system, at each level of which democratic proportional representation would apply. Legislation was enacted in 1993–4 to replace the existing segregated local councils in white towns, Coloured townships, African locations, and rural areas by a new nonracial system of local government.[60] Wisdom may have suggested that the transition should be gradual, perhaps by turning existing segregated African and Coloured townships into wards of the dominant white local council and gradually increasing their representation on that body. But this was not politically possible because of ways in which the demands of Africans for political rights had been slighted in the past and because resentment over the provision of basic services had led to very widespread rent boycotts in many parts of the country.[61]

The government therefore decided on a radical two-step process. The first step was to suspend all existing elective local councils throughout the country and to replace them with negotiating forums nominated by the administrator of each province. On these would sit, in equal proportions, members both of the existing councils and of other hitherto unrepresented bodies such as civic associations. They were to redefine municipal boundaries and see to the registration of voters, after which, as a second step, elections would be held in the newly defined areas, again on a fifty-fifty basis. A three-tier plan was devised for the larger municipal areas such as Johannesburg and Greater Cape Town. There, the wards and local councils would fall under an overriding metropolitan council, which would control the rating system and manage the larger services such as water supply and transport.

The law provided for elections on a ratio of 60 to 40 per cent, the larger figure being for ward representation, the smaller for party, in recognition of the fact that a constituency system was imperative at that level. Local elections were held across most of the country on 1 November 1995 but were delayed until May 1996 in KwaZulu-Natal and the Western Cape on account of interparty quarrels and litigation. In general, the major parties fared better than the smaller ones, and local issues were often submerged in wards where party contests had not been held before. But the arrangement also gave scope for independent candidates, who generally stood either on tickets of protest or for parties with little strength in the ward contested.

The Constitutional Court criticized the New Text for not having spelled out the constitution of local government more fully in view of the centrality given to three-tier democracy in the thinking of the Constitutional Assembly as a whole. Its requirement that the categories of municipality defined in the Local Government Act should be defined in the constitution and that their taxing powers should likewise be included was subsequently incorporated in the Final Text.

E. The Courts and Certification

The Supreme Court of South Africa, a product of a rigorous blending of the Roman, Dutch, and English legal systems, had been much reviled in recent years because of the laws it had had to enforce and the mandatory sentences it had been required to impose in political cases. Particularly notable were the pass laws, which in peak years had led to well over half a million arrests annually, and the vicious legislation of 1960–76 that had totally destroyed the rights of detained persons and had led to the death, from suspicious causes, of many detainees.

Judges had been appointed by the state president on what often looked like political considerations. They were nearly all white and nearly all male. So the task of the Constitutional Assembly, by common agreement, was to free the judicial system from executive and legislative dominance, from its unrepresentativity, and from all influences that interfered with the rule of law.

A key institution to set change in motion was a judicial service commission, on which the law profession, the universities, and the Senate were all represented, their role being to advise the president on all judicial appointments – in the case of ordinary judges, by supplying a list from which the president would be required to make his choice.[62] A Supreme Court of Appeal with final jurisdiction in all save constitutional cases (which it was also competent to hear) took over the mantle of the earlier Appellate Division to receive appeals from the renamed high courts.

Provision was made for establishment of the Constitutional Court – not a restoration of the packed progeny of the Appellate Division Quorum Act (1955), which had laundered the Coloured community off the voters' roll, but a new body, which would also consist of eleven South African citizens, four of whom must have been judges prior to appointment; but academic as well as practising lawyers were now to be eligible for promotion to this body. It was to be the court of first instance in civil rights cases, but in practice its main task was to have final appellate jurisdiction in constitutional cases proper.[63] The plan of the NP and ANC to leave the nomination of constitutional judges to the president alone was scotched by the DP's intervention at Kempton Park in 1993.[64]

The Constitutional Court threw its first challenge to the politicians in June 1995 by handing down a judgment that made the death penalty ultra vires.[65] It later invalidated the KwaZulu-Natal draft provincial constitution on the grounds of incompatibility with the New Text.[66] But its most important role was its assignment to certify the New Text after its adoption by the Constitutional Assembly in May 1996. The uniqueness of this role has been stressed by the Constitutional Court itself, as well as by other commentators.[67] Its performance received widespread acclaim from the clear interpretation it gave to its assignment: not in any sense to devise and insist on constitutional principles *ab initio*, but to measure the New Text against the principles in the Interim Constitution, with which it was required, reasonably, to conform.

A Licence to Proceed

Here, then, was the main constitutional framework within which South Africa was to shape itself into a new 'rainbow nation' over which bluebirds fly. How good a beginning was it? Whatever else happened – and this went for the experienced 'oldies' as well as the novices – it had to be a massive learning opportunity. The new parliament that assembled in May 1994 consisted of 400 MPs and 90 senators, the vast majority of whom had no experience of parliamentary government. From the moment the Transkeian male members bought jackets and ties, and their wives new hats, for the opening, it has been a story of overturning old conventions and learning new ones. Strictures on dress went, though not completely. Instead of referring to 'the honourable member for so-and-so,' MPs (who now had no earned constituencies) commonly referred to one another by name, with or without the endearing 'Comrade.' Audiences in the gallery, who had been condemned to total inactivity in the old days, now clapped, cheered, and interjected as vociferously as the backbenchers on the floor, or rose to their feet when Madiba walked in or spoke.[68]

Informality of a different order was replicated in committees, of which the most important were the standing portfolio committees of the two houses, which were concerned with day-to-

day legislation, and the six theme committees meeting simulta-
neously, which reported, through a larger committee with its
own executive subcommittee, to the Constitutional Assembly.
For the first time, all committee proceedings were thrown open
to the public, who were encouraged to submit memoranda,
make formal oral or written representations, and attend the
proceedings.[69] They were not encouraged to interrupt, nor were
they necessarily offered refreshments during the mid-morning
or mid-afternoon breaks, but it was easy for them to accost
members in an informal way. Because of the large number of
committees and the serious shortage of secretarial staff to
service them, daily order papers created extraordinary confusion from switches of time and place and as a result of the
frequent postponements because of overlaps and a resultant
absence of quorums.

There was reason to fear that the constitution building would
collapse from the sheer complexity of the process, but it did not
do so. The openness of the proceedings paradoxically provided
its own momentum. The seasoned constitutionalists, who were
concentrated mainly in the ANC, the NP, and the DP, managed
to maintain control and move the process along, with the help
of technical advisers, who achieved what must be described as
an immensely complex legal instrument, and with the aid of
literary consultants, who – on Canadian advice – combed out
a good deal of legalese at the cost of only minor grammatical
concessions.

Whether the structures created could sustain a workable
system of government still remained to be tested. Would the
electors – both those new at the game and those who were now
required to learn new values – show the sensitivity required to
build the culture of democracy on this challenging foundation?
Would the human resources of South Africa be able to sustain
a radically different and potentially much more powerful and
expensive provincial system and a much more representative

system of local government than had existed before? Would the country be able to sustain a revolution of rising expectations by balancing the costs of social salvage against the gains of economic revival? And could South Africa survive a tendency – which was very discernible in the closing stages of the Constitutional Assembly's debates – to break the truce of Joe Slovo's sunset clause and return to the battlefield of old-style party politics?

4

The Growing Pains of Democracy, 1994–1997

Trevor Manuel, minister of economic affairs and later of finance, attempts a difficult change of course from 'command' to 'social market' thinking, with opposition from other members of the ANC/SACP/COSATU alliance. (Cartoon by Zapiro. *Mail and Guardian*, 25 July 1996)

THE GENERAL ELECTION AND presidential inauguration of 1994 brought the new South Africa into being. The adoption of a democratic constitution at the end of 1996 gave it a legal identity. But the process of peacemaking, referred to in chapter 2, was not completed with the adoption of that new constitution in December 1996. There were tell-tale signs at the political level that consolidation still needed to happen.

The Government of National Unity, in which seats were shared on a pro rata basis by the African National Congress (ANC), the National Party (NP) and the Inkatha Freedom Party (IFP), took office with a firm commitment to waste no time in setting about the necessary repairs to South Africa's injured society. The time was certainly right when the former president, P.W. Botha, could actually telephone President Mandela to congratulate him on his election and when Mandela was able to carry out his own plan to meet with leading figures in the Afrikaner right-wing and National Party camps.

Mandela's intention was to coordinate a massive Reconstruction and Development Programme (RDP), orchestrated through the presidential office under the direction of a minister without portfolio, Jay Naidoo, who presented a white paper to the National Assembly on 15 November 1994.[1] Derek Keys, the minister of finance, aimed to cut inflation while aiming to find R2,116 million for health, welfare, education, housing, land, water, urban renewal, and other development projects, all of which would require an enormous sustained expansion of the economy.[2]

The strategy was imaginative. In the health field, it was to concentrate on primary health care by extending services into deprived areas, if need be by reducing subsidies to health services in the larger centres in the expectation that these could be covered by the expansion of private health care. In schooling, the plan was to combine the many different departments of the apartheid era into a single structure, though the system would still be administered through provincial subdepartments, and to replace uniracial schools and equalize the pupil-teacher ratios across the country in all areas and in all provinces while allowing private schools to continue. In the towns, the government proposed to redress the imbalance in the building of houses and allocation of services by combining existing ethnic local authorities into the single democratic nonracial structures provided for in the new Local Government Act. On the land, it would redress the enormous imbalance in land ownership and occupation that had developed for historical reasons, and at the same time it would build up a class of small farmers and create security from arbitrary eviction for labour tenants by enabling them to obtain title to land which they had occupied for long periods. It was the sort of program for which a Government of National Unity (GNU) was necessary if the nation was to pull together and succeed.

Its first hundred days elicited warm tributes but also important warnings. As Frederik van Zyl Slabbert, the former Progressive Party leader, put it, if a 'chicken in the pot before sundown' was the objective, they had better start looking for matches, firewood, a pot, and a chicken without delay. Nondelivery would be hard to justify once the promises negotiated in democratic trade-offs between parties to the GNU were in place and once the people were well drilled in what Sparks has called a culture of entitlement and protest.[3]

Doubts about the ability of the RDP to deliver were being expressed before the end of 1994 and continued afterwards.[4] These were often linked to the absence of adequate administrative organs at the provincial and local levels. This was true in the case of housing, where much had been achieved before the death on 6 January 1995 of Joe Slovo, the housing minister, despite disagreement between Slovo and Tokyo Sexwale, premier of Gauteng, over acceptable housing standards and despite a dispute between the ANC and the previous administration over who could claim the real credit for the policies adopted and the targets achieved. Local authorities were also hamstrung by a spread of rent boycotts, while funding companies were hit by bond-payment refusals across the land and by the growing trend of African squatters to move onto vacant land or – more provocatively – into houses allotted to other (often Coloured) occupants.[5]

In April 1995 Naidoo claimed substantial progress in the approval of housing subsidies, the electrification of homes, and the building of clinics, and in June a budget of R7,882 million was allocated, mainly for education, health, housing, land, and water affairs, with a discretionary allocation to the provinces. To meet the requirements of economic growth, the Industrial Strategy Project for improving manufacturing performance was launched by Trevor Manuel in June 1995. It focused on the defects of industrial management in the light of the deleterious effects of sanctions and the need to coordinate policy across the board. The new Growth, Employment, and Redistribution policy (GEAR) received pride of place in Manuel's first budget speech on 12 March 1997, with its emphasis on competitiveness, job creation and income spread, tariff reform, and private-public sector partnerships, all designed to improve productivity beyond the annual rate of 3.1 per cent that had been attained in 1996. To coordinate policy, a large team of experts was appointed to the deputy president's department, which had effectively taken over the management of the RDP.[6]

Industrial Tensions

On the industrial front in 1995 the unions, led by COSATU, continued to question the privatization strategy to which the government was cautiously committed. The unions wanted the state to be the coordinator of growth in preference to capitalist employers, whose aim to abolish exchange controls in order to improve their competitiveness in the world economy appeared to threaten the job market. The minister of labour, Tito Mboweni, responded to these fears with a new labour relations bill, which was designed to remodel the system that had directed labour relations ever since 1924.[7] Its aim was to replace statutory industrial councils with workplace forums and to limit the role of the more recent but controversial industrial courts. Although the Department of Labour had taken great pains to canvass overseas experience, the proposals were not easily accepted either by the workers or by business – especially by small businesses, many of which were not unionized. The trade unionists wanted mandatory industrial bargaining through shop stewards; they mistrusted agreements not enforced by law; and they insisted on the rigid exclusion of scab labour. The big employers threatened to pull out of negotiations rather than restore power to the unions, and both sides defied a ministerial deadline for agreement.[8] Despite all this, the negotiating parties recognized the needs of the RDP and responded positively when Mboweni intervened to break the logjam. They agreed to voluntary bargaining procedures and a minimal arbitral role for the state, yet left it to the government – through a recently created bargaining forum, the National Economic Development and Labour Advisory Council (NEDLAC) – to rule on the unresolved issues of scab labour and lockouts.[9]

Yet tensions continued through 1996 and 1997. Despite a notable decrease in working days lost through strikes between 1993 and 1995, and a lowering in the average levels of wage increases from around 14 per cent in 1986–90 to around 11 per cent in 1991–6, industrial unrest did not abate, and a major strike among textile workers early in 1996 saw the collapse of several firms after the employers had refused to back down from their compromise position.[10] Disagreement over the exclusion of a lockout clause in the new Bill of Rights during the drafting of the constitution led COSATU to picket the Constitutional Assembly – successfully. But having won the fight on the constitutional front, COSATU adopted a compromise position over the privatization issue in return for the right to be consulted in the negotiations.[11] This reflected COSATU's concern over industrial management as a consequence of sanctions, which had led it to support the Industrial Strategy Project. But it did not on that account lose its vigilance over conditions of employment; it staged a series of nationwide token strikes in support of its demand for a prescriptive forty-hour working week (against the offer of forty-five hours as an initial concession) and for more generous maternity benefits than business would concede, as amendments to Tito Mboweni's Basic Conditions of Employment Bill in 1997. Fired by GEAR's failure to deliver an expansion in the job market in its first year, COSATU, under Sam Shilowa's pugnacious leadership, gambled on its ability to force the employers' hands by persuading the ANC parliamentary majority to back its demands; but the ANC leadership, though conciliatory at the time of writing, remained committed in essentials to GEAR, which had recently received unequivocal endorsement from the governor of the Reserve Bank.[12]

Land Reforms

The RDP adopted a grandiose plan to place 30 per cent of all farmland in African hands within six years. This involved engaging three major holders of rights: the state, which held all land that had been placed under the Native Trust under the legislation of 1936; the traditional rulers, many of whom still held *dominium* over land on behalf of their subjects; and private (mainly white) landowners. The de Klerk government had legislated to make state land available in 1991; and in 1994, in order to induce Inkatha to take part in the general election, it had entered into a deal with the KwaZulu legislature, promising to place 95 per cent of the land of KwaZulu in the hands of the king as trustee on behalf of the chiefs. This greatly angered the ANC. A commission appointed by the GNU to investigate came under some pressure to reach an amicable consensus and decided to solve the problem with fresh legislation; but this was not likely to be a simple matter.[13]

In the case of privately owned land, the government took its first step with the Restitution of Land Rights Act of November 1994. This act set up a commission to investigate claims going back to 1913, the date of the first attempt at a nationwide segregationist land law. The new act laid down procedures for fair hearings and fair compensation to both parties and provided a land claims court to handle disputed cases.[14] Despite the emotional potential of land rights disputes, the measure did not produce the kind of outcry that many expected, essentially because of its emphasis on voluntary agreements wherever possible. Derek Hanekom, the minister, was criticized in some circles, and applauded in others, because by the beginning of 1997 very little land had passed from white to black hands – largely, it seems, on account of cost and administrative complexities, for many white-owned farms had been put on the market.

Far more contentious was the Land Reform (Labour Tenants) Act of 1995, which offered security of tenure to unpaid labour tenants who had a long occupation of land but no title to it. While protecting these tenants against pre-emptive evictions, the act enabled them, with financial aid from the state, to obtain title to a portion of the farm on which they worked, with a right to compensation if they left the farm for any reason.[15] Critics of the government's policy were mainly concerned to obviate the danger that uneconomic settlements might burgeon in the rural areas on land that was excised, with state money, from private property. The challenge to the ANC to justify the policy by setting up a large number of small farmers on the sequestered lands was entrusted to a deputy minister, Ms Thoko Msane, who was described by a discerning interviewer as being 'inexperienced, but resolute, well-informed ... and certainly not shy.'[16] There was scepticism aplenty in the farming community yet enough preparedness to give the new government some benefit of the doubt. Hanekom, who was normally engaging and conciliatory, had not worked well with Kraai van Niekerk, the NP holder of the Agriculture portfolio, and when the NP withdrew from the GNU, Hanekom added Agriculture to his Land Affairs portfolio, thus taking on the responsibility for productivity as well as redistribution. He soon announced a plan to dissolve the bureaucratic subsidy-providing control boards, which had spread into most sectors of farming since 1937, on the ground that they were a disincentive to competitive market-orientated farming. This move was widely though not universally welcomed.[17] A half-formed proposal by a treasury commission in October 1996 to introduce a land tax,[18] as well as advance notice from the minister of water affairs, Dr Kader Asmal, that he intended to break the age-old link between land ownership and water rights,[19] alerted the farming community to the dangers in these sensitive areas of policy.

A Return to Party Government?

The Government of National Unity (GNU) fell apart immediately after the initial passage of the Constitution Bill in May 1996 as a result of a defection – not by Inkatha, as might have been expected, but by the NP. After voting for the constitution, the NP withdrew from the GNU, the published reason being that its minority voice had not been able to make sufficient input into policy decisions to balance the loss of its public image as a party bound in a coalition.[20] De Klerk announced that the NP would take on the unfamiliar role of an opposition party. This was not to remove the protection of the sunset clause, which had broken the deadlock at Kempton Park in October 1992, because the GNU itself, however constituted, could be removed

only by a formal vote of no confidence, which was very unlikely to happen; but it was likely to encourage an immediate
return to confrontational politics.

The NP tried in late 1996 to float the idea of a new party that
would link all opposition groups and thereby ensure the sur-
vival of the two-party system. It saw itself as a custodian of the
culture of Afrikaans, which gave it a direct entry into the
Coloured community. This had enabled it to gain control over
the Western Cape. But by overtly wooing the Coloured people
it could not avoid alienating the African minority, many of
whom had looked forward to an ANC victory at the polls. The
NP also tried to woo Inkatha, and both sides had much to gain
from such a linkage – a racially mixed power base for the NP,
and white votes in Natal for Inkatha. But the NP had a past to
hide, Inkatha had too narrow a territorial base, and nothing
came of the bid.

Although the NP made considerable inroads into English-
speaking communities, where it was seen in numerical terms as
the only realistic opposition to the ANC, it could not shrug off
its past record simply by saying that it had committed an error
of judgment – a fact that cost it a great deal of support when
victims of the apartheid laws testified about their suffering
before the Truth and Reconciliation Commission (TRC). The
party therefore made no progress in its approach to the DP.

Sensing that the Afrikaans-language press was beginning to
turn against him, de Klerk transferred Roelf Meyer, the young
party leader who had steered the NP through the process of
constitution building, to a new post as party secretary in
February 1997 with the task of putting a new-look National
Party together. Meyer, not unpredictably, was soon insisting
that a realistic strategy had to begin with a dissolution of the
NP itself. This suggestion evoked a strong reaction from the
party's old guard, not least in the Western Cape, where it was
in control of the government. In May 1997 this element leaned
on de Klerk, who removed Meyer from his new post. Subse-

quently, Meyer left the party in a bid to start a new political movement. Within four months, de Klerk had fallen foul of the TRC and his party had initiated a lawsuit against it; Meyer had joined hands with Bantu Holomisa, who had received similar treatment from the ANC, to initiate a 'New Movement Process,' and de Klerk had withdrawn from politics altogether and handed over to a young party member chosen by the caucus, Marthinus van Schalkwyk.[21]

The Freedom Front could draw votes from NP ranks but from no other source. The DP, as the legitimate heir to the liberal political tradition in South Africa, had not been able to build constituencies outside the English-language professional and business classes. The PAC, whose policy statements, provocative propaganda, and occasional acts of terrorism had cut little ice with the electorate, underwent an unusual cosmetic change in December 1996, when Bishop Stanley Mogoba, who had formerly been a PAC member, agreed to become party president with a policy of his own that was rather closer to the Black Consciousness vision of Steve Biko and was linked to an explicit rejection of racism in the statement that 'Africa for the Africans' meant Africa for 'everyone, whatever their colour, who belong here, love their country and love their fellow-men and women.'[22] But this was not the sense given the following February in a press article by Bennie Bunsee, senior administrative assistant of the PAC, who projected the traditional PAC outlook, one with an ethnic rather than liberal or class dynamic.[23] There was clearly a deprived electorate 'out there' for the PAC to gather in – people unlikely to fall for the more restrained ANC brand of populism; but it could take time to draw them together, and if it succeeded it would overturn the cultural and political compromise of Kempton Park.

Meanwhile, with the constraints of an NP presence removed from the GNU, the ANC became more conscious of having to get its policies right and to consolidate relationships within the triple alliance, converting a marriage of convenience welded during the struggle into a partnership for a time of peace.[24] Thus, in July 1996 the government overhauled the work of the RDP, but in a manner that upset its officials because of the absence of previous consultation.[25] Jay Naidoo was transferred to Posts and Telecommunications, and a task force was set up under the supervision of Deputy President Thabo Mbeki, with three main purposes: to consider the redeployment of the RDP's functions to the line ministries in order to make them focus their budgeting more on development projects; to enable the government to subject development expenditure to financial discipline in face of the fall of the rand on world money markets; and to allow nongovernment organizations far more scope for participation in development than had originally been envisaged.

Although the RDP had so far failed in one particular task above all – the creation of more manufacturing jobs – it would be wrong to infer from the closure of the RDP office that the program had folded. The original targets were now tailored to more realistic goals, especially in the key areas of housing, education, and health. Budgeting was beginning to look at ways of drawing in private contributions – for example, by raising money from parents if their children's schools wanted to increase staffing or improve facilities above a given quota; by coordinating government and private housing projects; and by encouraging private medical aid schemes to carry the burden of costly hospitalization, leaving the state's hands free to pick up preventive medicine and primary health care. Alongside all this, an attempt was made to breathe more life into the Masakhane ('Let's build together') campaign, which had been launched in February 1995 by President Mandela to persuade people to end their rent and bond boycotts. The aim was to kill 'the Eighties culture of destroying state assets because they were part of the apartheid system' and to tell people 'that they must report on criminals for the sake of the community [and] take ownership of their communities.'[26]

In December 1996 the Mandela government released an internal assessment of its achievements, frustrations, and failures since the GNU had taken office.[27] On the credit side, it noted the establishment of a legitimate government in a free political system, the beginnings of an economic turnaround, and major reform in the provision of water, houses, and clinics for many (though not enough) of the needy. It deplored three crises, one in the Department of Health and two relating to damaging tensions within the party.

The first of these crises concerned the extravagant use of public funds by Dr Nkosazana Zuma, the minister of health, on a stage production generally judged to be of minimal value for a campaign against AIDS.[28] Zuma had reacted appropriately to investigation by the public protector but later announced that a private funder was prepared to remove the burden from the taxpayer – only to be told that anonymous donations were not acceptable for an official project of this kind.[29] The running of the Department of Health had always been difficult, and the problems of its transformation were so formidable that an ability to consult correctly and humbly was probably the qualification most needed in its head. The same could be said about the performance of Dr Sibusiso Bengu, minister of national education,[30] but this should not detract from the impressive performance of other departments singled out in this chapter. The ANC leadership was exposed to criticism largely because, although it was making bold efforts to restructure society on valid grounds, it had not mastered the routines and conventions of decision making in a complex political system.

The second faux pas noted in the ANC review was the expulsion from both the cabinet and the party of Bantu Holomisa, deputy minister of environmental affairs and tourism, who had earlier become president of Transkei by overthrowing the government of Stella Sigcau in a *coup d'état*, alleging that she had accepted a bribe from a financial magnate in return for dropping a court case against him.[31] Sigcau was now minister of public enterprises in the GNU, and Holomisa chose (without going through party structures) to denounce her to the Truth and Reconciliation Commission on a similar charge. The tension was increased when Winnie Madikizela-Mandela (the president's ex-wife) raised the issue in the ANC executive through Deputy-President Thabo Mbeki, arguing that Holomisa's dismissal, like her own, was bad for the image of the party.

Rank-and-file opinion in the triple alliance was at first mystified and then angered at the treatment of Holomisa. For his part, Holomisa fought a controlled campaign against dismissal but was unable to prevent it or even to retain his seat in the assembly because the constitution had placed the allocation of it in the hands of the ANC. He brought an action for wrongful dismissal against the party leadership; but as his case required him to retain ANC membership, which he was at first reluctant to abandon, he would have to bide his time before forming a rival party, which he clearly intended to do, when, in August 1997, he entered into a trial partnership with Roelf Meyer.

An equally damaging crisis arose in the Free State, where Patrick ('Terror') Lekota, the provincial premier, who had served seven years on Robben Island and later suffered four years' imprisonment after a mistrial for treason in 1987,[32] had aroused party anger by alleging corrupt practices by members of his executive. He faced a palace revolution in the Free State, where, although his popularity was high in the civic associations that had led the resistance in the 1980s, and also in the white electorate, it was relatively weak in the ANC, allegedly as a result of his rivals' fraudulent registration of new party members. The ANC national executive committee launched an inquiry but bought time by firing the entire Free State executive, including Lekota (without expressing a lack of confidence in him, though the provincial executive had done so) and then placing the province under an interim committee that was to hold office until a provincial congress – which was still to be convened – would make a decision.

In the meantime, Mandela announced that a place had been found for Lekota in the new National Council of Provinces (of which he was later elected president) and then selected Dr Ivy Matsepe-Casaburri, chair of the SABC board, to be the party candidate for the provincial premiership. Her selection was endorsed at a meeting called by the national executive and attended by members of the provincial legislature, by chairpersons and secretaries of Free State provincial regions, and by national organizers. It angered many members of the civic associations and was unsuccessfully tested in court by an ANC councillor before its formal endorsement in the legislature.[33]

The national executive's decision needs to be seen in the light of other undercurrents in the ANC cabinet. Thus, Mandela's replacement of Dr Pallo Jordan by Jay Naidoo (the former head of the RDP) as minister of posts and telecommunications, and Jordan's subsequent reinstatement as minister of environmental affairs reflected cabinet differences that ran deeper than a simple readjustment of portfolios after the NP withdrawal from the GNU.[34] The removal of Raymond Mhlaba, on grounds of incompetence owing to age, from the premiership of the Eastern Cape and his replacement by the Reverend Arnold Stofile was initiated by the national executive and later confirmed by the provincial party, in January 1997, without precipitating public protests against centrist intervention. But the national executive failed to ensure the re-election of Ngoako Ramathlodi, premier of the Northern Province, as provincial party leader, because its veto on the candidatures of Peter Mokhaba and Collins Chabane let in a rival, Senator George Mashamba, by a narrow margin in the caucus.[35] A similar tension showed itself in KwaZulu-Natal, where the national executive blocked bids by Senzo Mchunu and Sifiso Nkabinde, former office holders, from contesting top executive posts. Nkabinde, reputedly a 'warlord,' was later expelled from the party; his expulsion was shortly followed by renewed violence in the Richmond district (which

ANC supporters attributed to him).[36] These cases raised important questions about the calibre of ANC provincial branches to discipline themselves sufficiently to run a government, and about the ability of the ANC national executive, with the limited resources at its disposal, to manage the decentralization of power (required under the Interim Constitution) through structures of political control responsive to party discipline.[37]

The feeling that the president was sometimes inclined to take a stronger initiative than the constitution required had also surfaced over his public approval of Judge Ismael Mahomed to succeed Chief Justice Michael Corbett, before taking advice from the Judicial Service Commission; for the fact that the commission endorsed the nomination before Mahomed's formal appointment by the president meant that the alternative candidate could not have been recommended without a disagreement between the president and the commission becoming public.[38] A similar question is raised by the president's pointed grooming of Thabo Mbeki as his heir apparent in the presidency, which was countered by a denial that he was doing anything of the sort.[39]

From 1994 South Africa was admitted to the Organisation of African Unity and the Southern African Development Community (SADC); it was readmitted to the Commonwealth and was given the right to resume active membership of the United Nations. Like Smuts in earlier years, Mandela travelled to meet heads of state in Africa and the rest of the world, regularly inviting the foreign leaders to pay return visits. In association with India, he began to work for Third World representation on the Security Council. He made a personal impact on the politics of Africa, lecturing to Abacha of Nigeria and to Kabila of the renamed Congo – and also, in his capacity as their elected president, to the heads of the SADC – on their civil rights record. He also tried to promote effective southern African economic cooperation. The Hertzogian 'South Africa first' principle guided his dealings with the European Union as his government strove to enter the Lome Convention on equal terms with other African states. Realism, at the apparent cost of principle (but, in this instance, following the American lead), dictated a transfer of diplomatic ties from Taiwan to mainland China. Meanwhile, enormously profitable arms deals with the rival Arab states in the Middle East, which touched on another issue of principle, gave the country a toehold in a kind of business that was very good for job creation. These ventures aroused some parliamentary opposition, partly because of the government's reluctance to present is policies up front; but it would be difficult to demonstrate that the strategy of converting South Africa's diminishing polecat image into a bid for universal friendship did not enjoy the backing of the country as a whole.

The issue of bipartisanship invites a return to the question whether multiparty government was not still the best road for South Africa to take throughout the 'sunset' years to 1999 at least. In a country where a simple pattern of alternating governments was difficult to bring about, the reversion to open interparty confrontations on the parliamentary front was not the obvious route to follow in 1996–7, when parties directly responsible for past woes were beginning to crowd out the opposition benches. President Mandela saw the point. He made attempts at the end of 1996 to placate Inkatha, to the extent of making Chief Buthelezi, the leader of the only remaining coalition party, acting president for a few days on occasions when he and Deputy President Mbeki were both overseas.

The president also made a point of expressing his appreciation to all opposition parties at the opening of Parliament on 7 February 1997, and shortly afterwards he invited the PAC and the DP to discuss representation in the cabinet. However, both reached the conclusion that their existence as independent parties would be threatened if they responded positively to what could be construed as co-optations. In the case of the DP, it needs to be stressed that the invitation was taken as a compliment from Madiba. The federal council debated it very carefully, weighing the advantages of involvement in cabinet against the danger of losing the power of independent criticism, which the NP seems to have experienced in the Government of National Unity. The problem lay in lack of clarity over what lay behind the offer and the difficulty of seeing how a small minority in the cabinet could be effective if – as seemed to be the case from the report which the party leader Tony Leon gave of his interview with the president – majority votes would still determine cabinet decisions, complete cabinet confidentiality would apply, and independent criticism of policy decisions by the party would not be allowed.[40] Under such conditions, efforts at bridge building could well have been ineffective if not launched in a spirit of trust. How to build that trust at the human level was the last and surely the hardest of the divisions that needed to be overcome.

Truth and Reconciliation

Amid considerable controversy and after many meetings to ensure careful drafting, the Promotion of National Unity and Reconciliation Act was passed in 1994. In accordance with its terms, the president appointed the Truth and Reconciliation Commission (TRC) from a widely representative list of men and women, who were selected by a multiparty committee under the ANC lawyer, Fink Haysom, for their insight and human understanding.[41] Archbishop Desmond Tutu was given the chair of the TRC, and Dr Alex Boraine, past president of IDASA and a former Progressive Party MP, was made vice-chair. The work of the TRC was divided among three committees[42] – one on human rights violations, a second judge-controlled committee on amnesty,[43] and a third on reparation and rehabilitation.[44]

There had been a great deal of public debate, as was shown in chapter 2. The party negotiators accepted that the road to reconciliation had to include the laying bare of the wrongs of the past in a totally transparent agreement by those involved, including a full acknowledgment of guilt by the offenders, the offer of amnesty to those who made a full confession, and the grant of relief or reparation to those who had suffered a 'gross violation of human rights,' or to their survivors, including the victims of any successful applicant for amnesty.[45] The act defined a gross violation as 'the violation of human rights through ... the killing, abduction, torture or severe ill-treatment of any person ... or any attempt, conspiracy, incitement, instigation, command or procurement to commit an act referred to ... which emanated from conflicts of the past ... committed during the period 1 March 1960 to the cut-off date within or outside the Republic ... the commission of which was advised, planned, directed, commanded or ordered, by any person acting with a political motive.'[46]

An amended bill, placing rather more emphasis on the needs of the victims of violence, was passed into law in July 1995. It was at this level that most evidence was taken in the early months. Starting in April 1996, the human rights violation commissioners travelled extensively through the land, inviting testimony and obtaining from victims and other witnesses many grief-laden stories of family members who had been killed, shot, or tortured in police cells. At times the atmosphere became so charged with emotion that the proceedings had to be suspended. Witnesses were asked how the TRC could help them. Some wanted revenge, others compensation; others either wanted to know what had happened to their relatives or wanted the bodies back for proper burial – in one case, just the severed hand. Some, like the Biehl family, were prepared to forgive if they could only know whom to forgive and for what. Others – and this was particularly true of relatives of some of the better-known victims such as the Mxenges – insisted that justice must take its course, and they took steps to oppose amnesty applications to the TRC. They could not be given immediate answers until the hearings were completed and amnesty had been granted or refused.

Meanwhile, and more slowly, applications for amnesty began to come in towards the end of 1996. The applicants had to confess to common law crimes in the name of the state or a political organization, under a guarantee that the evidence, if satisfactory and full, could not be used in any criminal or civil proceedings against those whose admissions were accepted. Pardon was to be at the discretion of the judges in the amnesty committee, however, and could depend in terms of the Norgard principles on the severity of the crime.

The minister of justice, Dullah Omar, stated in May 1996 that the TRC would not prevent the courts from prosecuting people who had carried out massive human rights abuses in the apartheid era, that there would not be automatic amnesty for such offences, and that the operation of the TRC did not mean there would be no prosecutions; if *prima facie* evidence emerged against an individual who had not applied for amnesty, the attorney general would be bound to prosecute if a conviction was likely to be secured, not least for crimes of a political nature. If the amnesty committee refused an application for amnesty, the perpetrator could also be charged with a criminal offence.[47] On the other hand, should proceedings in the criminal courts and amnesty committee hearings coincide, the act laid down that the criminal proceedings could be interrupted by agreement between the TRC and the relevant attorney general. If amnesty was granted, proceedings were to become void forthwith, sentences were to lapse, and the person in custody was to be released immediately.[48]

Among the cases brought by the attorneys general that affected the TRC were those against Magnus Malan (former minister of defence) and nineteen others, which were heard between March and October 1996; against Eugene de Kock (who had been commandant of the Vlakplaas detention centre outside Pretoria), heard between March 1995 and October 1996; and against Dirk Coetzee (de Kock's predecessor at Vlakplaas), whose hearing started in July 1996.

In Malan's case, Attorney General Tim McNally of KwaZulu-Natal, who was thought by many to have shown little sympathy for human rights on previous occasions, failed to secure a conviction against any of the accused on charges of murder or of conspiracy to murder opponents of Inkatha. The failure of his case was so complete that it gave rise to allegations of deviousness and incompetence on the part of the prosecution, as well as complaints that the judge had failed to direct his mind to the performance of the defence counsels or the broader substance of the prosecution case.[49] After his exoneration, Malan at first stated that he had no intention of applying to the TRC, but he changed his mind after the TRC declared its intention to subpoena him, and he appeared before it in April 1997.

De Kock was convicted and sentenced on eighty-nine counts, including six of murder, several of attempted murder (including an attempt on the life of Coetzee), as well as arms offences and fraud. He was sentenced to effective life imprisonment. He subsequently testified at great length before the TRC, implicating two heads of state (P.W. Botha and F.W. de Klerk), three cabinet ministers, several leading generals in the army and police, and many lesser fry for authorizing, being involved in, or knowing of dirty tricks of one kind or another.[50] For his part, Coetzee disclosed a great deal of information about police third-force crimes before any case was brought against him. Soon after he appeared before the TRC, Attorney General McNally decided to put him on trial, and in April 1997 he was convicted of murder, along with others. The amnesty committee pardoned him on 4 August, before the court was due to pass sentence, to the chagrin of the family of Griffiths Mxenge, who reserved the right to have the case reopened in the high court.[51]

Lack of certainty over procedures and the risks involved in applying or not applying for amnesty caused widespread hesitancy among eligible applicants. This was particularly strong among senior officers of the old South African Defence Force (SADF), who were clearly encouraged by the result of the Malan trial. Their case was presented in October 1996 by Major General Deon Mortimer and General George Meiring, the current chief of the South African National Defence Force (SANDF). Their presentation was noteworthy for the blandness of its content. It described the action in Natal, which had provided the core of the case against Malan, as basically a response to a request from Buthelezi for support; it downplayed both the external and internal military operations of the SADF as routine; and it offered nothing on the Civilian Cooperation Bureau (CCB) – P.W. Botha's special force, which de Klerk had disbanded – beyond what had been released by the Harms Commission in 1992.[52]

In effect, the army had taken a stand on the legitimacy of its reaction to 'total onslaught,' and Constand Viljoen offered to take the rap for any atrocities committed by the SADF while it had been under his command – adding that he knew of no dirty tricks and that the CCB had not been in existence during his period in office.[53] The SADF's immunity may have been less secure than was thought, however, in view of the role of the CCB in certain 'dirty trick' operations and the impossibility of distinguishing between police and military action under the security structures set up under P.W. Botha's government. But at the time when the SADF gave its testimony, any hard justiciable evidence that might have been available was still under wraps, though it did not long remain so.[54]

In view of the close correlation of military and security police operations under the joint management councils set up by P.W. Botha, it would be wrong to draw a sharp distinction between the reactions of the army and the security police to the invitations and pressures of the TRC, for a distinction is often difficult to make.[55] But the security police's reputation for brutality was harder to conceal, despite the privacy extended to its investigative procedures under security legislation. It had operated under the direction of the State Security Council through the Counter-Revolutionary Intelligence Task Team, at least from the early months of 1986.[56] In January 1995 it was revealed that the minister of police, Adriaan Vlok, and some 3,500 policemen had applied for indemnity in terms of the Further Indemnity Act of 1992, shortly before the 1994 general election. There was a public outcry,[57] which was followed by a cabinet ruling that they had not received any immunity, and the legislation was repealed when the TRC was formed, though the individuals indemnified did not apparently lose the privilege.[58]

Twenty-two leading police generals decided to apply to the amnesty committee in June 1996. They included General Johan van der Merwe, the chief commissioner, as well as Johan Cronje and Dirk Coetzee (both former commanders of Vlakplaas who blew that organization's cover), Basie Smit, Johan Coetzee (architect of the detention-without-trial legislation), and Krappies Engelbrecht – all of whom declared their responsibility for several unresolved acts of terror.[59]

At first, individual policemen were slow to come forward, though some, like Dirk Coetzee and Craig Williamson,[60] had made early applications. Nearly all of those who applied were already imprisoned for offences committed or had been suspended from duty pending prosecution. But others were not in such a situation.[61] The decision whether or not to apply was difficult before the amnesty committee gave some indication of how it was going to interpret the rule that amnesty had to follow the accepted 'proportionality principle' under which the severity of the crimes committed had to be related to the political objective. It was a KwaZulu-Natal case that threw light on this. Brian Mitchell had already served part of a long prison sentence for his involvement in a security force operation against the United Democratic Front at Trust Feeds in Natal, when the wrong house had been attacked and innocent people killed. Mitchell received amnesty after he had made an emotional plea before the TRC for forgiveness, had joined the Rhema Christian sect, and had received an assurance from the community that it would support his application if he agreed to work for reconstruction. He was not granted amnesty for these reasons, however, but because his application fell within the terms of the Reconciliation Act.[62] Bona fide penitents could take reassurance from the Mitchell case. Mitchell subsequently returned to the community to seek its forgiveness.

Two further developments helped speed up the process: first, a threat by the TRC in August to subpoena individuals who did not come forward voluntarily; second, the president's decision to extend the period covered by the amnesty provisions to 10 May 1994. The threat of subpoenas caused many potential defendants to come forward, and some very frank statements, acknowledging responsibility in sensitive areas and a good deal of brutality, were made to the amnesty committee.[63] A few, however, like the former commissioner Johan Viktor (the founder of Vlakplaas), testified before the TRC without remorse.[64] By November 1996, the TRC had begun to receive applications from members of the SADF's 32nd Battalion, which consisted largely of Angolans who had previously fought against the MPLA; they sought amnesty for their role in random killings on trains on the Rand in the early 1990s.[65] The TRC had also been approached by men claiming responsibility for the murder of Steve Biko, the 'Cradock Four,' and the 'PEBCO Three.' In none of these cases had the courts so far been able to convict any individuals.[66]

The extension of the terminal date up to which criminal acts were eligible for amnesty to May 1994 was an incentive for white right-wingers and members of black movements that regarded themselves as being at war with the government to apply.[67] Constand Viljoen of the Freedom Front had urged this on behalf of Afrikaners who had been involved in acts of violence before the 1994 elections. The recommendation was backed by the ANC (which had at first been against it) and by Inkatha, whose self-defence units on the Rand were now inclined to bury the hatchet. Similarly, APLA saw the point of obtaining clearance for its earlier attacks on nonmilitary targets, but the DP was opposed to what it called an extension of the right to lawlessness. Mandela acquiesced, however. If his concession drew in township residents plagued by memories of necklacing, the concession could well be deemed worthwhile.

The effectiveness of the TRC depended not only on the response of individuals but also on that of the political parties. Here a distinction had to be drawn between submissions to the human rights violations committee, which could hear collective evidence, and applications to the amnesty committee, which could be made only by individuals. The NP application to the former body, presented by F.W. de Klerk, admitted very little blame. De Klerk stated, 'In dealing with the unconventional strategies from the side of the government ... from the outset within my knowledge and experience, they never included the authorisation of assassination, murder, torture, rape, assault or the like' – a statement that also covered the viewpoint of his colleagues.[68] P.W. Botha took a similar stand. At first, he refused to recognize the TRC, but in due course he agreed to talk to its chairperson, Archbishop Tutu, at a private meeting near his home on 21 November 1996, when he offered to cooperate, naturally on his own terms.[69]

The DP had no problems with the TRC – save that of trying not to appear self-righteous without ever having had the opportunity to misgovern. The Inkatha Freedom Party (IFP) presented a massive document, admitting no fault in its reaction to public violence, though Buthelezi apologized very broadly for any violence committed by IFP members. Guarded statements by Dr Jiyani, Inkatha's secretary general, and Dr F. Mdlalose, its national chairman, implied that the IFP would encourage its members to testify, but there was an obvious reluctance to do so. This was understandable, considering the extent to which its cadres were alleged to have been behind much of the violence of the late 1980s in association with security force units.[70] Brigadier Gqozo of Ciskei appeared before the TRC and apologized to the relatives of those killed at Bisho but claimed that the situation had passed out of his control.[71]

The ANC, presenting its case through Thabo Mbeki, tabled copies of its internal Motsuenyane and Skweyiya reports, which had looked into misdemeanours in its camps in exile before liberation, and named those executed there.[72] But it was slow to encourage individual members to come forward, at the same time leaning on the NP to admit the guilt of all, up to the highest political echelons, for crimes committed in the name of apartheid.[73] Nevertheless, Tom Lodge, the ANC's historian, as well as Koch and Edmunds, have characterized the ANC submission as 'both in its moral and academic integrity, far superior to that of the NP.' Meanwhile, there was no surge of individual ANC members applying for amnesty. But when the Transvaal attorney general announced that he planned to bring charges against some thirty-five ANC members in relation to the 1983 Church Street bomb blast in Pretoria, which had killed seventeen people, this prompted a last-minute rush by MK cadres to apply.[74] The minister of defence, Joe Modise, announced his intention to do so on 4 December, as did Ronnie Kasrils (deputy minister of defence), Sydney Mufamadi (safety and security), Jay Naidoo (telecommunications), and Mac Maharaj (transport). A meeting between Archbishop Tutu and Cheryl Carolus, deputy secretary general of the ANC, had cleared the air. There was, understandably, considerable resentment that the liberators should have to admit to guilt, but Archbishop Tutu threatened to resign from the chair of the TRC unless they did. The need for them to do so can hardly be overstated, just as it was important for the electorate as a whole to accept an obligation to offer compensation to the victims.[75]

The ability of the TRC to persuade human rights victims to accept what the state could offer by way of compensation had to depend on the work of the committee on reparations, whose options were bound to be limited by affordability in view of the many demands made for losses that were not identifiable as gross infringements of human rights.[76] Thus, if reconciliation was not to seem a hopeless quest, much would depend on the ability of the human rights and reparations committees to set the grievances and losses of the victims to rights, and of the amnesty committee to make disciplined yet humane assessments of the applications before it. Not all the victims were willing to forgive, and not all amnesty applicants appeared to express remorse. The more brutal members of the security forces often made less than complete submissions, or they justified their actions on the basis of orders received. Similarly, some liberating youths attributed their excesses, without regret, to encouragement from their leaders – a matter of hate speech leading to action. This is why the final task of the TRC, to produce a report on its findings for the benefit of posterity, could turn out to be very important.[77] To some extent, the human rights committee prepared the way for this when it extended its inquiries by inviting the press, the churches, education, the law, and other significant professions to explain their roles insofar as these helped to underpin or to undermine the inhuman structures of the past. Such a report, if it penetrates deeply enough into the social values of the various cultures that give quality to South African life, could provide the focal point for real reconstruction.

President de Klerk's National Party withdrew from the Government of National Unity immediately after the passage of the constitution, claiming that its contribution to policy making had been ignored. (Cartoon by Zapiro. *Sowetan,* 10 May 1996)

Notes

1: BREAKING THROUGH

1 Machiavelli, *The Discourses*, ed. Bernard Crick, tr. Leslie J. Walker
  (London: Penguin, 1970), 1:53 at 239: 'Turning now to the question of what it is easy and what difficult to persuade a people,
  this distinction may be made. Either that of which you have to
  persuade it looks at first sight like a sure thing, or it looks like a
  lost cause, or again, it may seem to it a bold thing or a cowardly
  thing to do. When proposals which have been laid before the
  populace look like sure things, even though concealed within
  them disaster lies hid, or when it looks like a bold thing, even
  though concealed within it lies the republic's ruin, it will always
  be easy to persuade the masses to adopt such a proposal. And,
  in like manner, it will always be difficult to persuade them to
  adopt a course which seems to them cowardly or hopeless, even
  though safety and security lie beneath it.'
2 Sheridan Johns and R. Hunt Davis, eds., *Mandela, Tambo and the
  African National Congress* (Oxford and New York: Oxford University Press, 1991) 183, 199, 281–93.
3 Steven Friedman, *The Long Journey: South Africa's Quest for a
  Negotiated Settlement* (Johannesburg: Ravan, 1993), 12.
4 The story is told in Allister Sparks, *Tomorrow Is Another Country:
  The Inside Story of South Africa's Negotiated Revolution* (Cape Town:
  Struik, 1994). For a responsible hatchet job on Sparks's journal-

istic skills from a careful historical perspective, see Christopher Saunders, 'The South African Transition: The Sparks Version,' *South African Historical Journal* 33 (1995), 216–24.

5 Sparks, *Tomorrow Is Another Country*, 15–20.

6 Ibid., 62–7. It involved transmitting coded computerized messages on public telephones via London to Lusaka, passing replies to Mandela on visits to prison in artfully practised handshakes, and recording his verbal replies by using a hidden pocket tape recorder.

7 *Mission to South Africa: The Commonwealth Report* (London: Penguin, 1986), 112; Sparks, *Tomorrow Is Another Country*, 34; Nelson Mandela, *Long Walk to Freedom* (Johannesburg: Macdonald Purnell, 1994), 517.

8 Brian Pottinger, *The Imperial Presidency: P.W. Botha, the First Ten Years* (Johannesburg: Southern Books, 1988), 332; Chester Crocker, *High Noon in Southern Africa: Making Peace in a Rough Neighborhood* (New York: Norton, 1992), 315–16.

9 Sparks, *Tomorrow Is Another Country*, 26–56; Mandela, *Long Walk*, 535–40.

10 J.E.H. Grobler, 'The ANC's Isolation of South Africa, 1960–1985' (unpublished paper, University of Pretoria, 1986).

11 Sparks, *Tomorrow Is Another Country*, 72–90.

12 Pottinger, *The Imperial Presidency*, 330, 404–7; Crocker, *High Noon in Southern Africa*, 304–16; E. Rhoodie, *P.W. Botha: The Last Betrayal* (Johannesburg: Melville, 1989).

13 See below, pp. 96 ff.

14 Sparks, *Tomorrow Is Another Country*, 91–102; R. Lawrence in S. Friedman and D. Atkinson, eds., *The Small Miracle: South Africa's Negotiated Settlement* (hereafter *Small Miracle*) (Johannesburg: Ravan, 1994), 7.

15 *South African Outlook*, Mar. 1990, 198–202.

16 Mandela, *Long Walk*, 543–5.

17 *South African Outlook*, Mar. 1990, 202–8.

18 *Race Relations Survey*, 1991–2, 498. Most had been lifted in 1990.

19 Friedman, *Long Journey*, 15; Sparks, *Tomorrow Is Another Country*, 129; *Race Relations Survey*, 1991–2, 72–3.

20 *Race Relations Survey*, 1991–2, 72, 466, 511.

21 *Race Relations Survey*, 1992–3, 473–87; Sparks, *Tomorrow Is Another Country*, 130.

22 Mandela, *Long Walk*, 588–9; Sparks, *Tomorrow Is Another Country*, 131–2; Friedman, *Long Journey*, 22–5.

23 Friedman, *Long Journey*, 24–55; *Race Relations Survey*, 1991–2, 557–8 (CODESA Declaration of Intent), and ibid., 1992–3, 499–508 (the activities of the working groups, which are also described in detail by Friedman, 34–128).

24 *Argus*, 24 Jan. 1992.

25 *Race Relations Survey*, 1993–4, 418–20; Sparks, *Tomorrow Is Another Country*, 133–4; Friedman, *Long Journey*, 40–2; Mandela, *Long Walk*, 590.

26 Friedman, *Long Journey*, 24–5, 34–58; *Race Relations Survey*, 1992–3, 499–503.

27 Friedman, *Long Journey*, 86–105; *Race Relations Survey*, 1992–3, 504–6.

28 Friedman, *Long Journey*, 108–28; *Race Relations Survey*, 1992–3, 506–7.

29 Friedman, *Long Journey*, 60–85; *Race Relations Survey*, 1992–3, 503. As background to the deadlock, the delegates also had to bear in mind the ineffectiveness of the entrenched two-thirds majority to protect the Coloured and African common roll franchise under the South Africa Act of 1909.

30 Friedman, *Long Journey*, 79–84. See also A. Reynolds, *Election '94 South Africa: The Campaigns, Results and Future Prospects* (Cape Town: David Philip, 1994), 3–10, for commentary by R. Mattes on the influence of opinion polls.

31 *Race Relations Survey*, 1992–3, 480.

32 Friedman, *Long Journey*, 74–6, 98–100.

33 Sparks, *Tomorrow Is Another Country*, 140–7; Mandela, *Long Walk*, 595; *Race Relations Survey*, 1992–3, 477; Friedman, *Long Journey*, 146. Sparks was an eyewitness of some of the events.

34 Sparks, *Tomorrow Is Another Country*, 140; Friedman, *Long Journey*, 148–52; Mandela, *Long Walk*, 596.

35 *Race Relations Survey*, 1992–3, 472.

36 Friedman, *Long Journey*, 106–28.

37 Ibid., 152–3; Sparks, *Tomorrow Is Another Country*, 148–52;

Mandela, *Long Walk*, 557. See also R. Kasrils, *Armed and Dangerous: My Underground Struggle against Apartheid* (London: Heine-
mann, 1993), 354–68, for views of this sacp buccaneer, who
became deputy minister of defence in the 1994 Government of
National Unity.

38 *Race Relations Survey*, 1992–3, 478.

39 Sparks, *Tomorrow Is Another Country*, 3–4, 179–96; Friedman, *Long
Journey*, 84–5.

40 Friedman, *Long Journey*, 145–6, 158–61; Mattes, in Reynolds,
Election '94, 11–13.

41 Friedman, *Long Journey*, 161–3; Sparks, *Tomorrow Is Another
Country*, 101–3.

42 Atkinson, in *Small Miracle*, 18–21.

43 *Race Relations Survey*, 1993–4, 528; Sparks, *Tomorrow Is Another
Country*, 187; Atkinson, in *Small Miracle*, 15–18. The right-wingers
were insistent on the drafting of a safe constitution before any
general election took place. Mattes indicates that the np cabinet
was deeply divided over the advisability of abandoning its association with Inkatha in favour of one with the anc (Reynolds,
Election '94, 13–17).

44 Sparks, *Tomorrow Is Another Country*, 187; Mandela, *Long Walk*,
602.

45 Later, information came to hand that the murderers might have
acted in collusion with opponents of Hani within the anc, but at
the time of writing this remained a matter of conjecture. See
report in *Sunday Independent*, 2 Feb. 1997.

46 Mandela, *Long Walk*, 601; Atkinson and C. Robertson, in *Small
Miracle*, 26, 45–6; Sparks, *Tomorrow Is Another Country*, 189. Chris
Hani was not allowed to become another Calvo Sotelo, but he
remained South Africa's Giuseppe Matteotti.

47 The Afrikaner Resistance Movement, a neo-Nazi political
movement that had played a provocative role in public affairs
since 1978. I was present at its first public demonstration,
when it tarred and feathered a Pretoria professor for challenging
the orthodox notion of divine intervention at the battle of
Blood River in 1838 when the Boers had taken revenge on the
Zulus.

48 *Race Relations Survey*, 1993–4, 29 (the Goldstone Commission's censure of the police for dereliction of duty); ibid., 1994–5, 141 (a departmental inquiry contradicting these findings). Viljoen later rose to the occasion in the restraint he showed over the revolution in Bophuthatswana and in his conciliatory contribution to the debate on the Shell House massacre, which was called by President Mandela in July 1995, on which occasion Viljoen spoke out against the culture of violence in a troubled society (see below, note 55).

49 The St James massacre, the assassination of Amy Biehl, and the wildcat shooting sprees of Barend Strydom and other lone white gunmen reflected sadly on the tensions in a changing society.

50 *Race Relations Survey*, 1993–4, 551; Sparks, *Tomorrow Is Another Country*, 194; Mandela, *Long Walk*, 603; Atkinson in *Small Miracle*, 34.

51 *Sunday Times*, 13 Mar. 1994.

52 At the urgent request of Mac Maharaj of the ANC, who had been sent to Mmabatho by Cyril Ramaphosa at the request of Roelf Meyer (Sparks, who was on the scene, 206–19).

53 Sparks, *Tomorrow Is Another Country*, 219.

54 Ibid., 219–24.

55 Mandela, *Long Walk*, 608. These events led to a political crisis in June 1995, when Mandela announced – not unreasonably – that, when approached, he had given the Shell House cadres permission to kill in self-defence; but the ANC was tardy to cooperate with a demand for a police inquiry. In a snap debate in Parliament, attended by the writer, Mandela railed against the actions of Inkatha without attempting to justify his own actions as he might have done, thus setting the tone of a debate in which, paradoxically, only black and white right-wingers made a plea for moderation (*Debates of the National Assembly*, 7 June 1995, cols. 2200–39).

56 Lord Carrington and Dr Henry Kissinger were the selected arbitrators. See also M. Cassidy, *Dawning of Democracy in South Africa: Stories behind the Story* (London: Hodder and Stoughton, 1994), 141–90, for a spiritual – and spirited – perspective on these events.

57 G. Hamilton and G. Maré, in Reynolds, *Election '94*, 82.
58 C. Robertson, in *Small Miracle*, 44–67.
59 Quoting Robertson, ibid., 53. See also S. Friedman and L. Stack, in *Small Miracle*, 302–7.
60 Schedule 1 of the constitution.
61 Under schedule 2 of the constitution. See also S. Friedman and L. Stack in *Small Miracle*, 301.
62 Friedman and Stack, in *Small Miracle*, 305–6.
63 Ibid., 308–10.
64 Ibid., 311–14.
65 Ibid., 316–21.
66 Under section 62 of the constitution.

2: PEACEMAKING

1 *Race Relations Survey*, 1993–4, 642–9.
2 For subsequent disclosures regarding third-force activities, see below, pp. 113n14.
3 *Frontiers of Freedom* (S.A. Institute of Race Relations), no. 4, 1995.
4 Steven Friedman, *The Long Journey: South Africa's Quest for a Negotiated Settlement* (Johannesurg: Ravan, 1993), 90–1.
5 *Race Relations Survey*, 1993–4, 507, and 1994–5, 120–3. See also Mark Shaw in S. Friedman and D. Atkinson, eds., *The Small Miracle: South Africa's Negotiated Settlement* (hereafter *Small Miracle*) (Johannesburg: Ravan, 1994), 228–56 (a very full treatment of the subject).
6 The Police and Prisons Civil Rights Union (POPCRU) had been formed in 1993 on the initiative of Gregory Rockman, an ex-SAP lieutenant, who had been dismissed from service for allegations of police brutality. See *Race Relations Survey*, 1991–2, 446–7, and 1993–4, 304.
7 *Race Relations Survey*, 1994–5, 428. See the full account of the military transformation by Mark Shaw, in Friedman and Atkinson, *Small Miracle*, 228–56.
8 See Mark Shaw, in *Small Miracle*, 204–27.
9 See *Race Relations Survey*, 1993–4, 660. Between January and June

1993, 109 policemen had been killed and 1,720 injured; 45 police stations and 516 police homes had been attacked, and 910 private (as distinct from public) police vehicles had been destroyed or damaged.

10 See below, pp. 100–2.

11 *South Africa: Torture, Ill-treatment and Executions in ANC Camps,* Dec. 1992, 1; *Weekly Mail,* 23–9 Oct. 1992. The Skweyiya Commission submitted to Mandela a confidential list of people (whom the *Weekly Mail* claimed to have identified), recommending their investigation by a fully independent body. The list was contested by the ANC, but reaffirmed by the *Mail* reporters in the issue of 30 Oct.–5 Nov. 1992.

12 *Race Relations Survey,* 1992–93, 32–3; *Weekly Mail,* 27 Aug.–2 Sept. 1993.

13 T.R.H. Davenport, *South Africa: A Modern History,* 4th ed., (London: Macmillan, pp. 545–6. According to the *Race Relations Survey,* 1988–89, 554, sixty-eight detainees died in police custody between September 1963 and August 1988.

14 See *South Africa: State of Fear: Security Force Complicity in Torture and Political Killings, 1990–1992* (New York: Amnesty International, June 1992); *Checkmate for Apartheid? A Special Report on Two Years of Destabilisation, July 1990 to June 1992* (Johannesburg: Human Rights Commission, 1992); Anthea Jeffery, *Spotlight on Disinformation about Violence in South Africa* (Johannesburg: SAIRR, 1992), which questions the above findings; and a series of papers by George Ellis (SAIRR, Cape Western Region) contesting Jeffery's definitions. Doubts about the existence of a 'third force' reflected in this debate were substantially laid to rest by evidence before the Truth and Reconciliation Commission and in court cases in 1996–7, as described in chapter 4. See also *Mail and Guardian,* 18–24 Mar. 1994 (report throwing light on the role of generals in gun-running), 25 Nov.–1 Dec. 1994 (the Pierre Steyn Report that was withheld by de Klerk), and 23–9 June 1995 (W.O. Paul Erasmus's revelations re the contents of that report). For Goldstone's revelations regarding police involvement in gun-running, see *Race Relations Survey,* 1991–2, 492–3.

15 *Race Relations Survey,* 1991–92, 492–3.

16 *Race Relations Survey,* 1992–3, 30–1, 37, 498–9; Friedman, *Long Journey,* 42–4. Not surprisingly, the Promotion of National Unity and Reconciliation Act of 1995 repealed the 1990 Indemnity Act, as well as the Indemnity Acts 124 and 151 of 1992, but it left the indemnities themselves undisturbed.

17 For the Constitutional Court's decision, see below, p. 58. See also *Sunday Times,* 11 June 1995 (articles by Ken Owen and Carmel Rickard).

18 For the TRC, see below, pp. 96 ff.

19 Friedman and Atkinson, in *Small Miracle,* 36–49.

20 *Argus,* 14 Sept. 1991; *Race Relations Survey,* 1991–2, lxiv, lxvii–viii. Two reporters described the attendance of 'more than a thousand' IFP supporters in red headbands, who were wielding traditional weapons, holding Buthelezi banners, and demanding 'genuine peace, not … another nice document in the filing cabinet signed in big hotels.'

21 *Race Relations Survey,* 1991–2, xxxiv. For the texts of all the main accord documents, see ibid., 1991–2, 522–56, and 1992–3, 123–4. See also *Argus,* 14 Sept. 1991 (D. Breier and C. le Grange).

22 See *Race Relations Survey,* 1993–4, 293–6; *Mail and Guardian,* 19–25 Aug. 1994.

23 The Commission of Inquiry Regarding the Prevention of Public Violence and Intimidation.

24 *Race Relations Survey,* 1992–3, 128, 462 (SADF attack in Thokoza township, Boipatong massacre); ibid., 1992–3, 465–6, and 1993–4, 188, 361–49 (taxi war in Western Cape, Alexandra, and elsewhere); ibid., 1992–3, 29, 245–6 (train violence); ibid., 1992–3, 29–30, 440–1 (Bisho massacre); and ibid., 1993–4, 643–4 (attack on the World Trade Centre).

25 *Race Relations Survey,* 1992–3, 28–9, 124 ff. (operations of Koevoet ['crowbar'], a combat unit in the Angolan war noted for its strong-arm methods); ibid., 1992–3, 31 (destabilization by military intelligence); ibid., 1993–4, 663 (KwaZulu-Natal violence); *Mail and Guardian,* 3–9 June 1994 (hit squad activity by KwaZulu Police units).

26 *Race Relations Survey,* 1993–4, 292–5.

27 *Mail and Guardian*, 19–25 Aug 1994, 12–23 Dec. 1996, and 24–30 Jan. 1997; *Sunday Independent*, 30 June 1996 and 19 Jan. 1997. See also below, p. 133n59.

28 *Weekly Mail*, 16–22 Mar. 1990 (reporter's interview with J. Battersby).

29 As an example of the former, see *Cape Times*, 29 Nov. 1991 (Tony Holliday), and of the latter, see *Weekly Mail*, 6–12 Sept. 1991 (Baruch Hirson). For shop steward membership of the SACP, see *Sunday Times*, 15 Dec. 1991.

30 *Cape Times*, 12 Feb. 1992, and *Weekly Mail*, 13–19 Nov. 1992 (articles by P. Stober and Jeremy Cronin). There were, however, signs of ideological hardening from 1994, in the wake of controversies over property rights and lockout provisions in the draft constitution, and at the ninth SACP congress in April 1995. See *Mail and Guardian*, 7–12 and 13–20 Apr. 1995, especially Mark Gevisser's interview with Dr Blade Nzimande.

31 See below, 81–3.

32 Derek Keys (executive chairman of Gencor, 1986–91), and later Chris Liebenberg (chief executive officer of Nedcor, 1990–4).

33 *Mail and Guardian*, 9–16 and 17–22 Sept. 1994. In 1995–6 the RDP was to run into rough water through bureaucratic inefficiencies and its failure to deliver on its promises in various fields.

34 Especially in the Abolition of Racially-Based Land Measures Act (1991) and its amendment (1993) and other related measures.

35 See *Weekly Mail*, 10–16 Jan. 1992 (Goedgevonden evictions), and *Mail and Guardian*, 4–10 Mar. 1994 (Boons expropriation); J. Krikler, *Revolution from Above, Rebellion from Below: The Agrarian Transvaal at the Turn of the Century* (Oxford: Clarendon, 1993), on British restoration to Boers of land reoccupied by blacks, after 1902; and L. Platsky and C. Walker, *The Surplus People Project: Forced Removals in South Africa* (Johannesburg: Ravan, 1985), on post-1948 expropriations.

36 This is not the place for a bibliographical introduction to the parties involved in the transition. Their roles are best seen in the works cited that handle the transition. Readers are referred, however, to the references in chapter 4 to the parties' dealings with the TRC. See below, pp. 96 ff.

37 See the discussion by S.T. van der Horst in Guy Hunter, *Industrialisation and Race Relations: A Symposium* (Oxford: Oxford University Press, 1965); Merle Lipton, *Capitalism and Apartheid: South Africa 1910–1986* (Cape Town: David Philip, 1986); and Deborah Posel, *The Making of Apartheid, 1948–61* (Oxford: Clarendon, 1991).

38 This is best seen in Steven Friedman's analysis of the CODESA working committees in his *Long Journey* and in the records of the Constitutional Assembly in 1994–6.

39 Johann van Rooyen, *Hard Right: The New White Power in South Africa* (London and New York: I.B. Tauris, 1994).

40 See *Race Relations Survey*, 1985, 38–43.

41 Tom Lodge, ed., 'The Poqo Insurrection,' in his *Resistance and Ideology in Settler Societies* (Johannesburg: Ravan, 1986), 179–222; C. Glaser, 'When Are They Going to Fight? Tsotsis, Youth Politics and the PAC,' in Philip Bonner, Peter Delius, and Deborah Posel, eds., *Apartheid's Genesis 1935–62* (Braamfontein: Ravan, 1993), 296–315.

42 G. van Niekerk, 'Return of the Prodigal Son: Some Prospects for a Revival of the PAC,' *International Affairs Bulletin* 12, no. 3 (1988), 35–64. For later developments, see below, p. 89.

43 See *Race Relations Survey*, 1991–2, 21–2; ibid., 1992–3, 473–4; ibid., 1993–4, 341–2; ibid., 1994–5, 522–3; and Davenport, *South Africa*, 378–9, 392–3, 426–7, for Black Consciousness and AZAPO.

44 Buthelezi's claim has been challenged, for example, by Mzala, in *Gatsha Buthelezi: Chief with a Double Agenda* (London: Zed Books, 1988), 102–15. See also Gerhard Maré and Georgina Hamilton, *An Appetite for Power: Buthelezi's Inkatha and the Politics of 'Loyal Resistance'* (Johannesburg: Ravan, 1987); and Davenport, *South Africa*, 376–8, 418–21, 426, 432–3, for general details on his career prior to 1990.

45 The entries on KwaZulu violence in the 1984 *Race Relations Survey*, referred only to faction fights (536–7); but from 1985 onwards the violence acquired a political dimension (for example, *Survey*, 1985, 292–3, 309–10, and 1986, 658–9). This suggests that the reasons for violence should be sought in the changes of the 1980s rather than in a long-standing hostility

between Zulu and Xhosa speakers, for which there is, admittedly, some evidence in the historical record. There was a remarkable cooling off of violence in KwaZulu-Natal in the run-up to the local government elections in mid-1996. This also suggests the possibility of centralized control.

46 *Weekly Mail*, 20–6 Apr. and 2–8 Aug. 1990, 19–25 July, 2–8 and 9–15 Aug., and 18–24 Oct. 1991, 10–16 and 24–30 Jan. and 30 Apr.–7 May 1992, 6–12 Aug. 1993; 22–26 July 1994, 17–23 Feb. and 24–30 Mar. 1995; *Sunday Times*, 7 May 1995, *Cape Times*, 13 June 1995.

47 See *Race Relations Survey*, 1991–2, 498 and 519–21, for the text of the ANC-IFP agreement of 29 Jan. 1991; see also Mandela, *Long Walk*, 582–3.

48 *Race Relations Survey*, 1992–93, 480. Given Buthelezi's normal stance that the king was a constitutional figurehead only, it is not easy to see why he insisted on his having a political role at CODESA in addition to that given to Inkatha.

49 See above, p. 19.

50 Notably by Professor Washington Okumu of Kenya.

3: CONSTITUTION MAKING

1 Leonard Thompson, *The Unification of South Africa, 1910–1960* (Oxford: Clarendon, 1960) was among the first to notice black opposition; and see especially Andre Odendaal, *Vukani Bantu! The Beginnings of Black Protest Politics in South Africa to 1912* (Cape Town: David Philip, 1984).

2 P.N.S. Mansergh, *South Africa 1910–61: The Price of Magnanimity* (London: Allen and Unwin, 1962; R. Hyam, 'African Interests in the South Africa Act, 1908–10,' *Historical Journal* 13, no. 1 (1970), 85–105; W.K. Hancock, *Four Studies of War and Peace in This Century* (Cambridge: University Press, 1961). The background to the debate lies in the promise made to the Boers in the 1902 peace treaty that there would be no early black enfranchisement, a promise confirmed in 1906–7 by the grant of self-governing constitutions to the Transvaal and the Orange River Colony. It has been argued variously, in justification of the British decision

not to veto the South African–made bill of 1909, that the Treaty of Vereeniging tied their hands, that a parliamentary system was suitable only for those out of whose culture one had emerged, or that (on the analogy of the American South) there was no effective constituency to safeguard the black vote should it be allowed. Great Britain was going through a crisis of conscience, in which it was of such paramount importance to do the right thing for the Boers that the blacks had to be asked to wait: let an enlightened white parliament enfranchise them in its own good time. 'We were children then,' commented Lord Brand (who had been secretary to the Transvaal delegation at the national convention) on a visit to Cape Town in 1960.

3 T.R.H. Davenport, *South Africa: A Modern History*, 4th ed. (London: Macmillan, 1991), 360–2.

4 Ibid., 280–7, 329–36, 342–3, 379–81.

5 Ibid., 383–4, 410–11, 428–37.

6 Ibid., 410–11; Gretchen Carpenter, *Introduction to South African Constitutional Law* (Durban: Butterworths, 1987), 287–8.

7 Interim Constitution, chap. 15.

8 Ibid., clause 229.

9 Ibid., clause 234.

10 Ibid., clause 235.

11 Ibid., clauses 236–8.

12 Ibid., clauses 238–40, 244.

13 Ibid., clauses 241–43.

14 Ibid., clause 245.

15 Ibid., clause 247.

16 S. Friedman and D. Atkinson, *The Small Miracle: South Africa's Negotiated Settlement* (hereafter *Small Miracle*) (Johannesburg: Ravan, 1994), 72, 97. Arthur Chaskalson and Marinus Wiechers had advised in Namibia.

17 I. Sarakinsky, in *Small Miracle*, 74–81, 104–17 passim.

18 D. Atkinson, in *Small Miracle*, 33, 82–9.

19 These principles were appended as schedule 4, which was linked to section 71 of the Interim Constittuion and could be amended or repealed only on appeal to the Constitutional Court, which was given the final say. See *Small Miracle*, 99–100. There were

thirty-three principles in the bill, but a thirty-fourth was added shortly before the 1994 election, under pressure from the Freedom Front, to keep open the possibility of group territorial autonomy.

20 Clause 73(1).

21 In the following pages, I use the term 'New Text' (following the terminology of the Constitutional Court for the final draft) for all drafts of the final constitution down to its adoption by the Constitutional Assembly, and I use the term 'Final Text' for the constitution as brought into force on 8 February 1997 after receiving the president's signature on 10 December.

22 South African Law Commission, Working Paper 25, Project 58, *Group and Human Rights* (1989) and *Interim Report on Group and Human Rights* (1991).

23 South African Law Commission, *Group and Human Rights*, 409, and *Interim Report*, 11.

24 National Party, 'Constitutional Rule in a Participatory Democracy: The National Party's Framework for a New Democratic South Africa,' Sept 1991, 4.

25 *Small Miracle*, 121–44; Interim Constitution, chap. 3; New Text, chap. 2.

26 *Certification of the Constitution of the Republic of South Africa: Judgement of the Constitutional Court*, 6 Sept. 1996 (hereafter *Certification*), 24.

27 The danger, as Dene Smuts argued in the debate on the film and publications bill, was that 'hate speech measures are always used by the powerful against minorities' (*Sunday Independent*, 8 Sept. 1996). This has often been shown, to the disadvantage of blacks, in the uses made of the hate speech clause of the Native Administration Act of 1927; to the disadvantage of non-Afrikaners, in various *boerehaat* outbursts in earlier white elections; and with lethal results for blacks in the shooting sprees of Barend Strydom and others, and for whites from the lips of black youths seeking amnesty for their part in the St James Church massacre and the murder of Amy Biehl (see above, pp. 17–18).

28 *Certification*, 16–17.

29 Interim Constitution, s. 9; New Text, s.11. See *The State v. T.*

Makwanyane and M. Mchunu, ccт 3–95, 6 June 1995; and submission by Amnesty International to the Constitutional Assembly, 13 Feb. 1996.

30 A decision to legalize abortion under safeguards was taken in
the Termination of Pregnancy Act of November 1996.

31 Interim Constitution, s. 27 (4) and (5).

32 *Certification*, pp. 20–1.

33 Constitutional Assembly, *Theme Committee 6, Workshop on Land
Rights and the Property Clause, 1–2 Aug. '95.* Note especially
papers by Derek Hanekom; by M. Chaskalson, Shadrack B.O.
Gutto, and Heinz Klug (all three from the Faculty of Law, University of the Witwatersrand, arguing against a property clause);
by the S.A. Property Owners' Association (arguing for one); and
by Antonie Gildenhuys (of the Human Rights Commission
arguing for a flexible clause). The House of Traditional Leaders
of KwaZulu-Natal sought the retention of the Ingonyama Act,
which conferred trusteeship on the king of the Zulus on behalf
of traditonal leaders (see p. 88).

34 *Debates of the Constitutional Assembly*, 28 Mar. 1996, cols. 312–13
(M. Smuts) and 408.

35 New Text, s. 29(2) (language in education), s. 30 (language and
culture) and s. 35(3)(k) (language in court).

36 *Sunday Times*, 7 Apr. 1996 (article by Mary Metcalfe, minister of
education and culture, Gauteng province); *Cape Times*, early Apr.
1996 (letter by Sibusiso Bengu, minister of Education). But for
the Freedom Front, as General Viljoen explained (*Debates of the
Constitutional Assembly*, 1996, cols. 433–5), denial of the Afrikaner's right to 'a greater measure of control over Afrikaans single-
medium schools' was the crucial issue that induced the party to
abstain from voting on the New Text of the constitution.

37 *Race Relations Survey*, 1992–3, 445 (Venda), 489 (Transkei), 1993–4,
633–7, and 1994–5, 341 (Bophuthatswana and Ciskei). Schedule 2
and ss. 235–47 of the Interim Constitution contained provisions
to guarantee continuity in all areas of government in independent homelands not yet incorporated, until these were systematically transferred to the Government of National Unity. Reconciliation of homeland laws with South African law was later tackled

by the Government of National Unity, in terms of complex provisions in the constitution, South Africa being redefined as a single territory of nine provinces that embraced all the homelands (see Map 1).

38 Atkinson, in *Small Miracle*, 102–7, who argues nevertheless that the compromise allowed the majority party to control the executive.

39 *Debates of the Constitutional Assembly*, 29 Mar.–8 May 1996, cols. 103, 250. Eglin drew particular attention to the chapter on cooperative government (ss. 40–1), a formulation both unique and necessary, especially for the interrelationship of government at national, provincial, and local levels.

40 Ibid., col. 251 (Eglin).

41 Atkinson, in *Small Miracle*, 109. The stranglehold which the anti-defection clause can have on the political behaviour of MPs was dramatically shown in May–August 1997 when a split occurred in the NP and the party rebel Roelf Meyer had to vacate his seat.

42 Thompson, *Unification of South Africa*, 97–109.

43 Ibid., 106–7.

44 New Text, ss. 213–30. There seems to be plenty of room for debate on the affordability of federal government and the impact which these constitutional arrangements could have on the balance between competing levels of spending – and taxing! Nicoli Nattrass (in *DSA in Depth* [an IDASA publication], Aug.–Sept. 1993, 28–30) saw federalism as a 'recipe for fiscal disaster' because of the difficulty of coordinating development finance so as to benefit the whole as well as the parts. Simon Barber (in the *Sunday Times*, 8 May 1994) saw it as a likely source of conflict between the different levels of government in their rivalry for the resources of the state, which would lead to increasing decentralization of governmental activity.

45 The ANC policy documents referred to 'real' government by the people rather than stressing lower house dominance. See the discussion documents 'Constitutional Principles and Structures for a Democratic South Africa' (April 1991) and 'Ready to Govern' (May 1992). The former, in providing for a senate, saw it as the 'guardian of the constitution' but its creation as an 'open question' (4, 23).

46 *Race Relations Survey*, 1993–4, 503.

47 See Interim Constitution, ss. 60–5, which provide for various categories of delegate: permanent delegates to attend all sessions, special delegates chosen ad hoc by the provincial premiers, and representatives of local authorities on a nonvoting, part-time basis, as provided for under s. 163.

48 Ibid., schedules 4 and 5.

49 S. 126 of the Interim Constitution, revised as s. 104 of the New Text. See Humphries et al., in *Small Miracle*, 151–4, 167–9, for the German background of this term.

50 Interim Constitution, s. 65, based on the German Bundesrat. See *Mail and Guardian*, 10–16 May 1996, 27 (Dennis Davis).

51 *Cape Times*, 16 Oct. 1996 (Patrick Bulger). The Constitutional Assembly amended s. 146(2) and (4) of the New Text by removing the presumption that a national law *must* prevail over a provincial law, save where this is *necessary* for dealing with an issue of national importance, leaving the matter for the courts to decide.

52 *Small Miracle*, 163–6; and see Map 2.

53 *Debates of the Constitutional Assembly*, (1996) vol. 1, col. 434.

54 *Race Relations Survey*, 1987–8, 922; ibid., 1988–9, 122; ibid., 1989–90, 510, 515–16, 676, 713; ibid., 1991–2, 498; ibid., 1993–4, 542. CONTRALESA had helped to set up ANC branches in Natal, enlisting at least one member of the Zulu royal house, which antagonized Buthelezi to such an extent that in September 1994 he brazenly invaded and broke up a live broadcast in the SATV studio in Durban in which that member was taking part (*Cape Times*, 28 and 29 Sept. 1994).

55 Constitutional Assembly, *Delegates to ... Public Hearing on Traditional Authorities, 12–13 May 1995*. In all, 178 attended. The titles given do not appear to be consistent, but they included 6 kings (all Eastern Cape), 3 paramounts, 7 princes, 64 chiefs, and others in various capacities, of whom 15 were women.

56 Information from Chief Phaketile Holomisa, president of CONTRALESA.

57 New Text, ss. 211–12, and Council of Traditional Leaders Act, 1997, s. 4(1)(c).

58 *Cape Times*, 8 Oct. 1996.

59 See references in note 44 above and the comments by Richard Humphries et al., in *Small Miracle*, 159–63, on the KwaZulu legislature's Constitution of the State of KwaZulu-Natal, adopted in December 1992, in which very extensive decentralization of power was indicated – short of outright separatism. Buthelezi had interpreted the status of the Zulu monarchy in accordance with the political situation at various times. He had forced the king to accept a nonpolitical role when the NP was using him to foist independence on KwaZulu in the 1970s. But he demanded representation both for the king and for the KwaZulu government at CODESA. He then reduced the king to a figurehead again when he crossed swords with him over participation in the 1994 general election, even to the point of asserting that one needed to distinguish between the institution of the monarchy and the person of the king.

60 Local Government Transition Acts, 1993 and 1994.

61 Every issue of the *Race Relations Survey* between 1985 and 1994–95 contains a substantial entry related to the boycotting of rent and service charges in African and other townships. See the 1994–5 *Survey*, at 534, for a calculation that the cumulative payment arrears since 1984 amounted to R1.84 billion.

62 New Text, s. 178.

63 Ibid., s. 167.

64 Atkinson, *Small Miracle*, 111–14. The judicial service commission had to be consulted over the appointment of the top Appeal and Constitutional Court judges.

65 *Sunday Times*, 11 June 95 (Carmel Rickard). This decision took some courage in view of the steep rise in the crime rate, but it must be seen against the very high incidence of death sentences handed down by the courts in the past. A strong campaign both inside and outside Parliament to secure the restoration of the death penalty in 1996 was ineffective.

66 *Race Relations Survey*, 1995–96, 437–8. The 'Kingdom of Kwa-Zulu/Natal' was described in the first draft as a 'federate' province of the Republic of South Africa, with characteristics verging on independence, a separate citizenship, and an executive endowed with powers of law enforcement that could not be made

to mesh with the reshaped security forces of the Republic. In face of strong opposition from the ANC and DP, Inkatha revised its approach after talks with the NP; but it still could not satisfy the Constitutional Court.

67 'It is necessary to underscore ... that the basic certification exercise involves measuring the NT against the CPS. The latter contain the fundamental guidelines, the prescribed boundaries, according to which and within which the CA was obliged to perform its drafting function ... There is a distinction to be made between what the NT may contain and what it may not. It may not transgress the fundamental discipline of the CPS; but within the space created by those CPS, interpreted purposively, the issue as to which of several permissible models should be adopted is not an issue for adjudication by this Court. The Court is concerned exclusively with whether the choices made by the CA comply with the CPS, and not with the merits of those choices ...' (Certification, 6 Sept. 1996, 11). See also Prakash Naidoo (in the Sunday Independent, 8 Sept. 1996), who discussed these issues in the light of the international debate over the propriety of a nonelected court having the final say on the validity of a constitution adopted by a properly accountable legislature. The elected representatives had in fact handed over this power to the court. The principles against which the draft had to be tested were products of an ad hoc assembly constituted under the old order; but because they were formulated in very general terms, it could be argued that they required professional elucidation, provided that the court refrained from being prescriptive, which – in the words quoted above – it certainly tried to avoid being.

68 During the debate in June 1995, following Mandela's statement that he had given the ANC cadres in Shell House permission to shoot to kill if Inkatha marchers attacked their party headquarters in March 1994, the ANC claque in the galleries was too vocal for the Speaker to control – if, in fact, she tried. Madiba is Mandela's clan name.

69 The pile of public memoranda shown me in one MP's office, governing Bill of Rights questions, stood a metre high.

4: THE GROWING PAINS OF DEMOCRACY, 1994–1997

1 *Sunday Times,* 22 May 1994 (Edyth Bulbring).

2 *Mail and Guardian,* 24–30 June and 26 Aug.–1 Sept. 1994; *Cape Times,* 7 Sept. 1994; *Business Day,* 16 Nov. 1994.

3 I draw on *Argus,* 13–14, 17 Aug., and 30 Nov. 1994 (David Breier, F. van Z. Slabbert, and Stanley Uys); *Cape Times,* 13 Oct. 1994 (Allister Sparks).

4 See, for example, *Business Day,* 16 Nov. 1994.

5 *Mail and Guardian,* 15–21 July, 14–20 and 21–7 Oct. 1994 (Drew Forrest). For problems relating to housing, see *Mail and Guardian,* 15–21 July and 14–20 and 21–27 Oct. 1994 (Drew Forrest); and for RDP budgetary allocations, *Cape Times,* 25 Apr. 1995, and *Mail and Guardian,* 15–22 and 24–30 June 1995.

6 *Argus,* 25 Feb. 1997; *Cape Times Business Report,* 13 ar. 1997 (text of budget speech); *Mail and Guardian,* 16–22 May 1997 (Marion Edmonds on Mbeki; Hein Marais and Gavin Lewis on the RDP).

7 *Government Gazette* 356 (10 Feb. 1995). Draft Negotiating Document in the Form of a Labour Bill.

8 Views expressed by Clive Thompson, Glenn Adler, and Sam Shilowa (secretary general of COSATU), respectively, in *Mail and Guardian,* 3–9 Feb., 24–30 Mar. and 5–11 May 1995. See also *Cape Times,* 7 June 1995.

9 *Business Day,* 14 July 1995 (Renee Grawitsky); *Cape Times Business Report,* 21 July 1995 (Carl von Holdt); *Mail and Guardian,* 21–7 July 1995 (Andrew Levy).

10 For the textile strike, see *Cape Times,* 19 and 26 July; *Mail and Guardian,* 24–30 Mar. and 22–8 July 1996; *Argus,* 3–4 Aug. 1996. For the fall in working days lost, see *South African Survey,* 1995–6, 308–9; and for improved wage settlements, *Cape Times Business Report,* 27 Sept. 1996 (Thabo Leshilo).

11 *Argus,* 20–1 July 1996 (Estelle Randall). *Mail and Guardian,* 26 July–1 Aug. 1996 (Madeleine Wackernagel) and 20–6 Sept. 1996 (Max Gebhardt) show the shift in COSATU's position over time.

12 *Mail and Guardian,* 11–17 Apr., 8–14 Aug. 1997 (Azghar Adelzadeh in defence of deficit budgeting), and 15–21 Aug. 1997 (Sech-

aba Nkosi on COSATU's September report); *Cape Times Business Report*, 27 Aug. 1997 (defence of financial orthodoxy by the governor of the Reserve Bank).

13 Under the Ingonyama Trust Act of the KwaZulu legislature. See *Argus*, 21–2 May 1994; *Mail and Guardian*, 20–6 May and 27 May–2 June 1994; and *Race Relations Survey*, 1994–5, 103.

14 *Race Relations Survey*, 1994–5, 549–50; ibid., 1995–6, 363–7; *Sunday Times*, 29 May 1994; *Cape Times*, 30 Jun. 1994; *Argus*, 28–9 Jan. 1995; *Mail and Guardian*, 31 Mar.–6 Apr. 1995. See also *Mail and Guardian*, 11–17 Apr. 1997 (criticism of delays by Jim Day), and 25 Apr.–1 May 1997 (defence of land policy by Susan Lund); TRAC (newsletter of the Transvaal Rural Action Committee), Feb. 1997; and *Groundwork* (newsletter of the Border Rural Committee), Feb. 1997, for explanations of the complexities of transfer.

15 *Cape Times*, 29 June 1995; *Mail and Guardian*, 7–13 July 1995. Objections were raised, in particular, to the suggestion of ministerial discretion in the allocation of such land, as being a serious inroad into the rights of the existing title holders. A departmental green paper over Hanekom's signature in February 1996 attempted to allay these fears by promising flexibility in procedures still to be devised.

16 *Sunday Times*, 12 Feb. 1995 (Kevin Davie); *Mail and Guardian*, 4–10 Aug. 1995 (Mark Gevisser).

17 *Cape Times*, 14 Aug. 1996.

18 For example, *Cape Times*, 25 Oct. 1996.

19 *Cape Times*, 21 Nov. 1996; *Mail and Guardian*, 29 Nov.–5 Dec. 1996.

20 *Argus*, 9 May 1996. De Klerk said he would cease to be deputy president on 30 June and added: 'It would be unnatural to continue in the GNU while everybody knows the principles on which it rests have been discarded in the new constitution. The ANC is acting more and more as if they no longer need multiparty government.' Mandela reacted by saying the ANC was 'supremely confident that we are going to carry the government of this country ... I thank Mr De Klerk for his contribution.'

21 *Cape Times*, 12 and 20 Feb. 1997; *Sunday Times*, 16 Feb. 1997 (Ray Hartley); *Mail and Guardian*, 21–7 Feb. 1997; radio interview,

Roelf Meyer with John Maytham, 22 May 1997. For F.W. de
Klerk's resignation from politics, see *Argus* 26 and 27 Aug. 1997.

22 *Mail and Guardian*, 20–3 Dec. 1996 (Benjamin Pogrund on the
Thohoyandou congress).

23 *Cape Times*, 5 Feb. 1997. Bunsee argued: 'The resolution of the
national question is ... the dividing line of our politics [between
the ANC/SACP/COSATU and the PAC/AZAPO/BCM groupings] ... In
reality this divides the entire nation ... In dealing with the national question, the dividing line is whether we continue along a
Eurocentric road or transform the country on the basis of the
primacy of an Africanist/black identity. The implications of this
change are enormous and radical in their concepts. The ANC/
SACP/COSATU alliance ... wishes to effect an integration into
European culture but with socio-economic changes to benefit the
impoverished in our society ... The PAC and AZAPO, while want-
ing radical socio-economic changes, also want the fullest assertion of African/black identity. The land issue that is central to
their politics symbolises this viewpoint, although it does not
fully explain it. Demographically, this has great implications in
the radicalisation of the government and controlling institutions
and structures of society. It means a displacement of what we
have traditionally accepted. The approach to history and the
language issue will be treated differently. Representation will be
accompanied by a different content.' These words, hovering on
the borderline between cultural Africanism and black racism,
have great inflammatory potential when linked to the common
argument that deprived communities intent on the pursuit of
justice for themselves cannot be called racist. The issue came to
the fore in a much-publicized confrontation between Professor
Dennis Davis of Wits University and Barney Pityana, chairperson of the Human Rights Commission. See issues of the *Mail
and Guardian* between 8–14 March and 17–23 May 1996 (articles
by Davis, Margaret Legum, Justin Pearce, Peter du Preez, Mark
Gevisser, Frederik van Zyl Slabbert, and Laurie Nathan), taken
with an interview with Pityana in *Argus*, 30–1 Mar. 1996). See
also *Mail and Guardian*, 23–9 May 1997 (Marion Edmunds).

24 *Mail and Guardian*, 15–21 July 1994 (Paul Stober); *Sunday Times*, 27 Oct. 1996 (Ray Hartley).
25 *Mail and Guardian*, 12–18 July 2996; *Cape Times*, 22 July 1996 (Gavin Lewis).
26 *South African Survey*, 1995–6, 340; *Mail and Guardian*, 6–12 Sept. 1996 (Marion Edmunds). See also *Sunday Independent*, 9 June 1996 (Rod Amner), for examples of Masakhane's successes and failures.
27 *Sunday Independent*, 10 Nov. 1996 (Adrian Hadland, on the ANC's internal assessment of the GNU's record after thirty months in office).
28 On the later stages of the 'Sarafina 2' crisis, see *Sunday Times*, 25 Feb. 1996; *Mail and Guardian*, 9–14 and 22–28 Mar. (Mark Gevisser on Mbongeni Ngema and N. Zuma), 7–13 and 14–20 June 1996; *Argus*, 30 May 1996; *Cape Times*, 12 Sept. and 1 Dec. 1996.
29 *Mail and Guardian*, 31 Jan.–6 Feb. 1997. Criticism from outside the party focused on the running down of effective medical services in the larger centres, especially teaching hospitals; on the loss to the public service of many leading medical personnel through severance packages and the large-scale substitution of doctors from overseas; and the promotion of research into an anti-AIDS drug, Virodene, without the authority of the Medicines Control Council.
30 The Department of Education, with good reason, had decided to get rid of a grotesque imbalance in the spread of educational funding through the different ethnic departments, which had persisted since 1925, by amalgamating all departments into a single structure (administered provincially), abolishing racial segregation in all schools, and ensuring uniform pupil-teacher ratios and equal funding for schools across the board. This involved the relocation of large numbers of teachers in the better-supplied provinces and severance packages (to be paid for by contributions from overseas if these could be obtained) for teachers who rejected relocation. Several thousand teachers were declared redundant in Gauteng and the Western Cape on the eve of the 1997 school year, even though assessments of teacher needs in several provinces, including the affected ones, had not

been properly made and sufficient money to fund severance had not been obtained. The minister announced on 10 February 1997 that redeployment was therefore to be deferred but not cancelled. Extra costs to cover the salaries of those not transferred crippled departmental finances (*Cape Times*, 18 Sept. 1997). A group of Cape schools, some of which had lost experienced teachers through severance, won a case against the minister in 1997 for the right to appoint teachers on merit without having to accept candidates at the head of the transfer list – an action vilified by some as being racist and made on political rather than sound educational grounds. Again in 1997, a new general syllabus based on the challenging principles of outcomes education had to be hurriedly deferred because many teachers had not had the time to prepare for it.

31 For the dispute between Bantu Holomisa and the ANC, see reports and comment in the *Cape Times*, 23, 24 May, 13 June, 28 Aug., and 2 Oct. 1996; *Mail and Guardian*, 2–8 and 16–22 Aug., 6–12 and 13–19 Sept., 1–7 and 18–24 Nov. 1996; *Sunday Times*, 6 Oct. 1996.

32 *Race Relations Survey*, 1989–90, 167–8.

33 On the Free State ANC crisis, see reports and commentary in the *Sunday Times*, 27 Oct. 1996; *Sunday Independent*, 10 Nov. 1996; *Cape Times*, 11, 15, 27 Nov. and 2 Dec. 1996; *Mail and Guardian*, 2–8 Aug., 8–14 and 22–8 Nov., and 29 Nov.–5 Dec. 1996.

34 *Mail and Guardian*, 4–11 and 12–14 Apr. 1996; *Cape Times*, 14 May 1996.

35 *Sunday Independent*, 8 Dec. 1996, *Cape Times*, 9 Dec. 1996.

36 *Mail and Guardian*, 6–12 Dec. 1996.

37 Ss. 128 and 141 of the New Text made the election and dismissal of provincial premiers dependent on simple majority votes in the legislature, replacing the two-thirds majority required for dismissal in the Interim Constitution, ss. 145–6.

38 See *Mail and Guardian*, 20–6 Sept. 1996. The interview of the two applicants for the post, which I witnessed, was conducted with scrupulous formality. There was no obligation on the president's part to do more than listen to the commission's advice with regard to this judicial post (as opposed to others); but the confi-

dential advice of the responsible professional body should have
been regarded as a sufficient guarantee for the general public,
for whom a relationship between the head of state and the senior judicial body ought normally to be seen as a relationship of
trust.

39 This may be behind the criticisms of Mbeki by Tokyo Sexwale,
premier of Gauteng. See *Sunday Times*, 29 Sept. 1996.

40 *DP Despatch*, 2, 4 (16 Feb.–10 Mar. 1997). A personal comment may
be appropriate here. In 1955 I took part in a debate in the national
executive of the Liberal Party in Johannesburg to discuss an invitation from the Congress Alliance to take part in the Congress of the
People at Kliptown, at which the Freedom Charter was presented
for public support. The meeting listened to a presentation by Peter
Beyleveld of the Congress of Democrats and after a long discussion turned it down, on a divided vote, because it was felt that
the invitation should not have been made at the last minute by an
organization against which the party had very recently been
engaged in elections for African seats in Parliament and the Cape
provincial council, especially as that movement still had a Stalinist
agenda in the era of the cold war. The element of trust was
missing when there had been no confidence build-up between
the Congress Alliance and ourselves. In retrospect, had we
received a clear picture of the Freedom Charter and the manner
in which it had been devised – the widespread canvassing of
opinions even in remote rural areas and the submission of
grievances from many ordinary people (some of them 'written
on brown paper'), and the essentially moderate terms of the
Charter itself – the story could well have been different.

With Mandela's offer of 1997, the same degree of mistrust was
not present. There was the problem of how to achieve solidarity
in a cabinet that had not been built around a pre-election coalition, with its ministerial pattern previously sorted out and the
limits of consensus carefully defined. But the mere fact that both
the ANC and the DP had committed themselves in spirit to a 'new
South Africa' protective of human rights in an open social-mar-
ket economy suggests that the door half-opened by Mandela had
not in fact been closed. A meeting of the Western Cape provin-

cial council of the DP (which I also attended) a week before the
federal body, had given a strong indication of support for join-
ing the government if the right conditions could be worked out.

41 *Mail and Guardian*, 12–18 May 1995 (Gaye Davis notes 130 hours
of committee sessions and over 300 amendments before the
Promotion of National Unity and Reconciliation Bill emerged as
an agreed measure).

42 The TRC was required 'to establish as complete a picture as
possible of the causes, nature and extent of the gross violations
of human rights ... committed during the period from 1 March
1960 to the cut-off date, including the antecedents, circumstances, factors and context of such violations, as well as the
perspectives of the victims and the motives and perspectives of
the persons responsible for the commission of the violations ...;
establishing and making known the fate or whereabouts of victims and ... restoring the human and civil dignity of such victims
by granting them an opportunity to relate their own accounts of
the violations ... and ... recommending reparation measures in
respect of them; completing a report providing as comprehensive
an account as possible of the activities and findings of the commission ... which contains recommendations of measures to
prevent the future violation of human rights.' See Promotion of
National Unity and Reconciliation Act, 1994, s. 3(2)(a), (c), (d).

43 The 1994 bill stated that any person seeking amnesty for deeds
associated with a political objective could be granted a hearing
behind closed doors and be required to disclose all relevant
facts. Names of those granted amnesty, and the acts pardoned,
would be made public. Should the amnesty seeker be charged
with an offence, the committee could 'request the appropriate
authority to postpone the proceedings pending the consideration
and disposal of the application for amnesty,' and the amnesty
seeker would be protected against civil or criminal proceedings
in respect of any act for which amnesty had been granted.

In the 1995 legislation there was a much tighter definition of
the term 'political objective,' which had to link the applicant to a
'publicly known political organization or liberation movement'
engaged in a struggle with an explicit political organization or

its security forces; there was explicit exclusion of acts committed for personal gain or out of 'personal malice, ill-will or spite' (s. 20 passim). Public hearings were laid down as the norm, and confidential hearings were to be held only in special cases at the committee's discretion (s. 33). The compromise was allowed at the request of the minister of justice (*Cape Times*, 1 Feb. 1995).

44 To recommend to the commission 'any such steps as would be reasonable having regard to available resources ... to grant restitution or rehabilitate the applicant.'

45 See Alex Boraine and Janet Levy, *The Healing of a Nation?* (Cape Town, 1995), and the review by Gerhart Werle in *Democracy in Action* 9, no. 2 (Apr. 1995); and Peter Mayende, 'Pitfalls of the Truth Commission,' MPD *News* 3, no. 4 (Dec. 1994). At a workshop at the University of Cape Town attended by the writer on 11 March 1995, speakers stressed the importance of disclosure for therapy to be effective, and they looked for 'a contextual understanding of the particular historical processes, patterns of social relationships and institutional dynamics relevant to the perpetration of gross human rights violations during this period.' In a public lecture in Cape Town on 6 February 1997, also attended by the writer, Judge Goldstone laid special emphasis on the importance of individualizing guilt if truth procedures were to make an impact on people.

46 Act 34, 1995, s. 21(8).

47 Quoted by Eddie Koch in the *Mail and Guardian*, 26 Apr.–2 May 1996.

48 Act 34, 1995, s. 21(8).

49 Information and comment on the Malan case from *Mail and Guardian*, 1–7, 8–14, 22–8 Mar., 28 June–4 July, 18–24 Oct., and 29 Nov.–5 Dec. 1996; *Cape Times*, 12, 24, 26 Sept., 10 Oct., and 28 Nov. 1996 (Justice Minister Omar's criticism of McNally); *Sunday Times*, 13 Oct. 1996; *Argus*, 4–5 May and 30 Nov.–1 Dec. 1996. The last *Mail and Guardian* reference suggests that the prosecuting authorities, had not yet rediscovered the skills needed to press home charges in political cases now that third-degree methods used against state witnesses in the apartheid era had been outlawed. The second *Argus* reference summarizes an article 'Failing to Pierce the Hit-Squad Veil: An Analysis of the

Malan Trial,' by Howard Varney (convener of the investigative
unit that handled the prosecution case) and Jeremy Sarkin of the
University of the Western Cape, which was to appear in the
March 1997 issue of the *S.A. Journal of Criminal Justice* and which
severely criticizes both the prosecuting counsel and the judge. I
am grateful to Professor Sarkin for letting me see this article.

50 *Cape Times*, 31 Oct. 1996; *Mail and Guardian*, 30 Aug.–5 Sept.
1996. For de Kock's testimony to the TRC, see *Mail and Guardian*,
5 Sept. 1996; *Cape Times*, 17, 19, 23 Sept.; *Sunday Times*, 22 Sept.
1996. The TRC still has to react to his appeal.

51 *Cape Times*, 5 Aug. 1997.

52 *Cape Times* and *Star*, 1 Nov. 1996.

53 *Cape Times*, 7 Feb. 1995.

54 See below, pp. 102 and 135n65.

55 Davenport, *South Africa*, 397–8; Annette Seegers, *The Military in
the Making of Modern South Africa* (London: I.B. Tauris, 1996),
268–86.

56 *Sunday Times*, 27 Oct. 1996 (Marlene Burger).

57 *Weekly Mail*, 30 Oct.–5 Nov. 1992; *Cape Times*, 13, 16, and 18 Jan.
1995; *Argus*, 14–15 Jan. 1995; *Sunday Times*, 22 Jan. 1995.

58 Unity and Promotion of National Reconciliation Act, 1995, s.
48(1) and (2); *Mail and Guardian* 16–22 Feb. 1996 (Jacko Maree, NP
member of the justice subcommittee). The 1990 Indemnity Act
had offered amnesty 'for the sake of reconciliation and for the
finding of peaceful solutions' and had led to the release of
thousands of prisoners. That of June 1992, in response to an ANC
demand for the release of 350 named prisoners, extended
amnesty to prisoners who might 'promote reconciliation and
peaceful solutions' and led to the freeing of 168 long-term,
mainly ANC prisoners. After the April 1994 elections, the minister
of justice appointed the Currin committee to handle pending
amnesty applications. It secured the release of 160 prisoners,
some of whose applications had previously been rejected, some
of whom had been sentenced for nonpolitical offences, and all of
whom were ANC sympathizers. Some high-profile ANC members,
among them Thabo Mbeki, Joe Modise, and Pallo Jordan, had
not yet had their re-entry indemnities renewed.

59 *Cape Times*, 25 and 26 June 1996; *Sunday Independent*, 30 June

1996 and 19 Jan. 1997; *Mail and Guardian,* 17–23 Dec. 1996 and 24–30 Jan. 1997. These police officers had all been recommended for dismissal or suspension by General Pierre Steyn in a report to de Klerk shortly before the 1994 election. The Steyn Report had been commissioned after Judge Goldstone had followed a lead given to the police (who disbelieved it) by a disgruntled Mozambican deserter. But de Klerk, who claimed only to have listened to a verbal statement by Steyn, kept some of these policemen in office, including van der Merwe; and for the sake of not destabilizing the country on the eve of the 1994 general election, he kept the report under wraps, in due course providing President Mandela with a copy.

60 For Williamson, see *Cape Times,* 20 Feb. 1995; *Sunday Times,* 26 Feb. 1995; *Mail and Guardian,* 24 Feb.–2 March 1995 and 16–22 Feb. 1996.

61 *Mail and Guardian,*26 July–1 Aug. (Eddie Koch), 16–22 Aug. (Stefaans Brummer), and 20–3 Dec. 1996 (Eddie Koch).

62 *Sunday Times,* 15 Dec. 1996 (Carmel Rickard). Mitchell qualified because he was a 'member of the security forces or a known political organization or liberation movement'; his action had been ordered by his superiors, its motivation was linked to a political struggle, and its 'proportionality' was seen as being within acceptable limits; he had aimed to eliminate named individuals even if he had hit the wrong ones; and Mitchell had made a full disclosure of the relevant facts. The TRC made it clear that it would not be sufficient for him to claim amnesty on the basis of membership of unknown organizations or to have acted simply from private ideological impulses.

63 See, for example, *Star* 1 Nov. 1996 (W.O. van Vuuren, Jack Cronje); *Cape Times,* 4 Nov. 1996; *Sunday Independent,* 10 Nov. 1996 (Dirk Coetzee); *Cape Times,* 13 and 29 Nov. 1996 (Leonard Knipe, Dolf Odendaal, Johan Kleyn, Supt. William Liebenberg, and others, all of the Western Cape police, subpoenaed by the amnesty committee). Captain Jeff Benzien gave the amnesty committee a practical demonstration of the wet bag method he had used to bring political prisoners to the brink of suffocation – and in one instance beyond it (*Cape Times,* 15 July 1997). Eddie

Koch argued (see *Mail and Guardian*, 25–31 Oct. and 20–3 Dec. 1996) that the plan of those who came forward may have been to admit as little as possible to the TRC and then avoid cross-examination, so as to maximize the protection afforded under the act.

64 *Cape Times*, 19 Nov. 1996.

65 *Mail and Guardian*, 29 Nov.–5 Dec. 1996 (Peter Thorneycroft and Eddie Koch). For the debate on the third force, see above, p. 113n14.

66 The security police had been exonerated in the inquest on Steve Biko. But in September 1997 five of the eight security policemen who had held him in custody applied for amnesty, admitting to culpable homicide but not murder (*Mail and Guardian*, 5–11 Sept. 1997). The Cradock Four (Matthew Goniwe, Sicelo Mhauli, Fort Calata, and Sparow Mkhonto) had been murdered in 1985, and their deaths attributed by the presiding judge – after the reopening of an unsatisfactory inquest – to unidentifiable members of the security forces; but five other security policemen arranged to appear before the amnesty committee in October 1997, one of whom had given a public account of the events in June (*Argus*, 6–7 Sept. 1997). The PEBCO Three from Port Elizabeth (Sipho Hashe, Champion Gasela, and Qawaquli Godolozi) had simply disappeared without trace, but it emerged that their bodies had been thrown into the Fish River.

67 The decision was controversial. See *Cape Times*, 20 Aug., 2 Sept., and 23 Oct. 1996; but contrast *Mail and Guardian*, 8–14 Nov. 1996. The TRC, took the suggestion seriously, and on 13 December Mandela told General Viljoen and Dr Alex Boraine, deputy chairman of the TRC, that he would ask Parliament to extend the amnesty to 10 May 1994. The DP was opposed to the extension. The ANC had been firmly opposed, but pressure from members of ANC self-defence units and Inkatha self-protection units on the Rand, which were willing to bury the hatchet, made a rethink by the cabinet a possibility. APLA then decided to urge its members to apply (*Cape Times*, 12 Dec. 1996; *Argus*, 14–15 Dec. 1996; *Mail and Guardian*, 13–19 Dec. 1996). The president assented to the extension.

68 *Mail and Guardian*, 23–9 Aug. 1996 (Eddie Koch and Marion

Edmunds, quoting de Klerk's document); *Cape Times*, 2 Sept. 1996 (Sandile Dikeni). While apologizing for apartheid in general terms, de Klerk again denied knowledge of any NP decision to authorize criminal violence for political ends, in a further presentation to the TRC. See *Cape Times*, 15 and 16 May 1997. When Archbishop Tutu expressed public disappointment at de Klerk's reaction, claiming that de Klerk had told him differently in private, the NP, later backed by the IFP, threatened a court action to demand an apology from Tutu and the removal of Boraine from the TRC. Although there was no provision for a collective admission of guilt by any party, leading to a grant of amnesty, it can hardly be gainsaid that a forthright and explicit acceptance of blame by the leaders of political parties whose followers had been involved in serious rights infringements could only have helped the conciliation process.

69 For the Tutu-Botha interview, see *Cape Times*, 22 Nov. 1996. In a written statement, Botha is reported to have said: 'I am not guilty of any deed for which I should apologise or ask for amnesty. I therefore have no intention of doing this.' He denied that the bombing of Khotso House, which he was reported to have authorized, was a 'gross violation of human rights,' and he asked Archbishop Tutu to provide him and his former ministers with a list of aspects on which it wanted clarification. This, according to the *Argus* of 4 Feb. 1997, was subsequently done.

70 *Argus*, 9 May and 6 Sept. 1996; *Cape Times*, 20 and 21 Nov. 1996.

71 For new evidence on the Bisho shootings, see *Argus*, 9 May and 6 Sept.'; *Cape Times*, 11 Nov. and 3, 5, 8 Dec. 1996.

72 See above, pp. 32 and 113.

73 *Cape Times*, 23 Aug. 1996.

74 *Mail and Guardian*, 20–6 Aug. 1996; *Cape Times*, 11 Nov. and 3, 5, 8 Dec. 1996. Deputy President Thabo Mbeki led an ANC delegation to the TRC in May 1997, admitting ANC responsibility for a number of specific acts of violence, including the Church Street bomb blast. See *Cape Times*, 13 May 1997.

75 *Cape Times*, 12 Nov. 1996. (Roger Friedman). The Reparation and Rehabilitation Committee of the TRC tabled a policy framework of five categories for urgent intervention: emotional, material,

medical, symbolic, and educational infringements. Relief was to be borne by a presidential fund. A joint committee of both houses of Parliament was to advise the president on urgent measures, the final document to be in the government's hands early in 1997. The document accepted that 'if the state is to grant amnesty to perpetrators of human rights violations, it is under obligation, within available resources, to provide for reparations to victims and survivors.'

76 *Cape Times*, 29 Jan. 1997. R450 million was set aside for 1997 pay-outs to freedom fighters, with parliamentary approval. It was recognized by the minister of lands that payment of monetary compensation for loss of land rights could seriously limit the resources needed for development.

77 Peter Storey was right to ridicule the suggestion that 'there was any moral equivalence between fighting to maintain white Afrikaner dominance ... and struggling to free South Africans of all races from oppression ... [But] it is ethical nonsense to argue that all the deeds done in its name had equal moral weight because of the morality of the struggle ... That is the very trap the truth commission was set up to avoid' (*Sunday Independent*, 10 Nov. 1996).

Index

Page numbers in italics refer to the notes.

African National Congress
(ANC), 9, 14–15, 32, 34, 37–8,
43, 51, 53, 57, 59, 63–5, 81, 89,
92, 102, 121
Afrikaner Broederbond, 7
Afrikaner paramilitary movements (AWB etc.), 17, 18, 27,
42, 110
Afrikaner rights (language, *volkstaat*), 39, 42, 49, 55, 59–61, 64,
68–70
Afrikaner Volksunie, 53
agriculture. *See* land policy
amnesty and indemnity, 32, 33,
64, 96, 114, 132–5
APLA. *See* Pan-Africanist Congress
Asmal, K., 87
Azanian People's Organization
(AZAPO), 43; AZANLA, 28

Barnard, N., 6

Bengu, S., 91
Biehl, A., 18, 97, 111
Biko, S., 44, 102, 135
Bill of Rights, 13, 54–61, 71. *See
also* rights
Bisho, 15, 19
Bizos, G., 6
Black Consciousness, 28, 43, 89
Boiphatong, 14
Bophuthatswana, 12, 15, 18, 53,
61
Botha, P.W., 5, 6, 7, 50–1, 81, 99,
100, 103, 136
boycotts: rent, and 'Masakhane'
campaign, 43, 72, 83, 90; trade,
3, 27, 37
Bunsee, B., 89, 127
Buthelezi, M.G., 14, 44–5, 71, 95,
116, 117

cabinet, 22, 52, 61–2
Carolus, C., 104

Carrington Lord, *111*
Castro, F., 4
China, People's Republic of, 95
Ciskei, 12, 15, 19, 53, 61
Civil Cooperation Bureau, 100
civic associations (SANCO), 43, 92–3
CODESA. *See* Convention for a Democratic South Africa
Coetsee, Kobie, 5–6
Coetzee, D., 98–9, 101
Coloured people, 40, 50, 88
Commonwealth: Eminent Persons' Group, 6; return to, 94
Concerned South Africans Group (COSAG), 16
Congress of South African Trade Unions (COSATU), 14, 37–8, 43, 59, 83–5
Congress [Council] of Traditional Leaders (CONTRALESA), 45, 70–1, *122*
Conservative Party (CP), 41, 53
constitution, 49, 63, *117–18*; 1960, 49; 1983, 49–50, 61; Final, 73, *129*; Interim, 13, 20, 34, 52–4, 57, 61–2, 64, 70; New Text, 23, 55–6, 57, 59, 62, 63, 65, 71, 87, *119*, *121*
– anti-defection clause, 62–3; Bill of Rights, 13, 54–61, 71; cabinet, 22, 52, 61–2; concurrent powers, 54–5, 64–5, *122*; deadlock, 65; entrenchment, 13; open government, 62, 75–6; political parties, role of, 52, 62,

103; presidency, 13, 52, 56, 61, 81; proportional representation, 20, 62; referenda, 11, 13, 51; representativity, 55, 74; 'sufficient consensus,' 53; sunset clause, 16, 17, 37, 87. *See also* constitutional principles; federalism; homeland reincorporation; National Council of Provinces; regionalism; Senate
Constitutional Assembly, 54, 57, 58, 59, 76, 84
constitutional principles, 34, 54, 58–9, 61, 64, 70
CONTRALESA. *See* Congress of Traditional Leaders
Convention for a Democratic South Africa (CODESA), 10–14, 15, 34, 51
Corbett, M., 10, 94
courts and justice, 52, 55, 73–5, 94, *129*; Constitutional Court, 34, 52, 57, 58, 59, 65, 73–5, *124*; Judicial Service Commission, 74, 94
Cradock Four, 102
Crocker, C., 4
cultural autonomy, 55, 59
customary law, 70

death penalty, 58, 74, *123*
de Klerk, F.W., 4, 7, 8, 9, 10, 16, 18, 33, 40, 41, 51, 61, 88–9, 100, 103, *126*, *136*
de Kock, E., 98–9
de Lange, P., 7, 34
Democratic Party (DP), 40–2,

52–3, 57, 59, 62–3, 74, 88–9,
95–6, 102, 103, 130–31
detention: ANC camps, 32; South
African, 32, 73

economic policy, 36, 83–5. *See
also* Government of National
Unity; Reconstruction and
Development Project
education policy, 5, 52, 60, 82–3,
90–1, 120, 128–9
Eglin, C.W., 61, 121
elections: 1994, 17, 20–2, 35, 43,
45, 81; 1999, 62
Erwin, A., 38
external relations, 94–5

federalism, 54–5, 63–5, 121. *See
also* National Council of Provinces; regionalism
finance, 52, 54, 55, 63. *See also*
Growth, Employment, and Redistribution Policy
Freedom Front, 42, 70, 89
Free State (OFS), 5, 92

gender commission, 58
Goldstone, R., 35–6
Government of National Unity
(GNU), 3, 19, 23, 34, 40, 53,
61, 81, 87. *See also under*
economy, education, health,
housing, labour, and land
policies
Gqozo, J., 19, 103
Groote Schuur talks, 9
Growth, Employment, and

Redistribution Policy (GEAR),
83, 85

Hanekom, D., 86–7
Hani, C., 16, 37, 110
Harms Commission, 33, 100
health policy, 81–2, 90–1,
128
Holomisa, B., 89, 91–2
homeland reincorporation, 12,
15, 61, 120–1
housing policy, 82–3, 90–1

Independent Electoral Commission, 12, 20–1
Inkatha (IFP), 10, 16, 19–20, 28,
34, 44, 53, 64, 70–1, 81, 85–6,
88, 103

Kasrils, R., 15, 104
Keys, D., 81
Kriegler, J., 20
KwaZulu-Natal, 15, 22, 44–5, 61,
70, 71–2, 74, 101, 123–4

Labour Party, 11
labour relations and policy, 37,
58, 82, 84. *See also* Congress of
South African Trade Unions;
strikes and lockouts; trade
unions
land policy, 38, 85–7, 115, 126
language rights, 59–61
Law Commission, 56
Lekota, P., 92
local government, 43, 52, 55,
72–3

Madikizela-Mandela, W., 6, 9, 92
Maharaj, M., 104
Mahomed, I., 94
Makwetu, C., 11
Malan, M., 98–100, 132–3
Mandela, N., 3, 4, 6, 7, 8, 9, 10, 16,
    17, 18, 34, 45, 51, 81, 94, 95, 102
Mangope, L., 18
Manuel, T., 38, 83
Mass Democratic Movement, 8,
    43, 45
Matseppe-Casaburri, I., 93
Mbeki, T., 7, 34, 61, 62, 90, 92,
    95, 104
Mboweni, T., 84–5
McNally, T., 99
Mdlalose, F., 103
Meiring, G., 100
Meyer, R., 15, 88–9, 92, 111
Mitchell, B., 101–2, 134
Modise, J., 104
Mogoba, S., 89
Mortimer, D., 100
Motsuenyane Report, 32, 104
Mufamadi, S., 104
Mxenge family, 97, 99

Naidoo, J., 8, 90, 93, 104
National Assembly, 62, 65, 75–6
National Council of Provinces
    (NCOP), 64–5, 122. See also Sen-
    ate
National Economic Development
    and Labour Advisory Council,
    84–5
National Party (NP), 8, 39–40, 51,
    56, 59, 63, 81, 85, 87–9

National Peace Accord, 34–5,
    114
Nkabinde, S., 93

Okumu, W., 19
Omar, D., 98
Organisation of African Unity, 5,
    94

Pan-Africanist Congress (PAC), 9,
    11, 16, 17, 28, 30, 43, 53, 89,
    95; Azanian People's Libera-
    tion Army, 28, 102
Peacemaking, 27–9, 81
PEBCO Three, 102
police: SAP, 31, 112–13, 134–5;
    SAPS, 31
provinces, 13, 20, 64, 66–7, 74–5.
    See also National Council of
    Provinces
public opinion polls, 14

racism and antiracist propa-
    ganda, 89, 105
Ramaphosa, C., 15, 111
Ramathlodi, N., 93
Ready to Govern, 14–15
Reconstruction and Development
    Project, 38, 81–3, 85–7, 90
Record of Understanding, 16, 48
referenda, 11, 51
regionalism, 13, 64. See also fed-
    eralism
rights: of association, 57;
    cultural, 55, 59; freedom of
    speech, 57, 119; children's,
    58; group, 56; horizontal, 57;

language, 59–61; life, 58; property, 59, *120*; women's, 58, 71. *See also* Bill of Rights

St James massacre, *111*
Self-defence units, 28, 102
security forces, 29–32, 99, 100, 102
Senate, 13, 14, 52, 56, 64. *See also* National Council of Provinces
Sexwale, T., 82
Sharpeville, 23
Shell House shootings, 19, *111*
Shilowa, S., 85
Sigcau, S., 91–2
Sisulu, W., 8, 11
Skweyiya Commission, 32, 104, *113*
Slabbert, F. van Z., 41, 82
Slovo, J., 16, 17, 37, 82
South African Communist Party (SACP), 5, 9, 14, 37, *115*
Southern African Development Community, 94
Soweto, 5, 28–9
Sparks, A., 5, 11, 82
State Security Council, 100
Steyn, P., 36, *113*, *134*
Stofile, A., 93
strikes and lockouts, 14, 38, 58–9, 84

Terre'Blanche, E., 17
third force, 28, 33, 35, 45, *113*
total onslaught, 100
trade unions, 14, 55, 83–5
traditional leaders, 52, 55, 64,

70–1, *122*. *See also* Congress of Traditional Leaders
Transitional Executive Council, 11, 53
Transkei, 12, 28, 61
Treurnicht, A., 40
triple alliance (ANC, SACP, COSATU), 14, 37–8, 42–3, 89–90
trust feeds, 102–3
Truth and Reconciliation Commission, 7, 40, 58, 96–105, *131–2*
Tutu, D., 96, 103, 104, *136*

Umkhonto we Sizwe (MK), 9, 10, 17, 28, 104
United Democratic Front, 43, 101–2
United Nations, 94

van der Merwe, J., 101
van Niekerk, K., 87
van Schalkwyk, M., 89
Venda, 12, 61
Viktor, J., 102
Viljoen, C., 17, 18, 42, 70, 100, 102, *111*
violence, 4, 23, 27–9, 35, 45, 102; taxi wars, 28; on trains, 102
Vlok, A., 101

water affairs, 87
Western Cape, 22

Zulu monarchy, 14, 19, 44, 45, 86, 117, *123*
Zuma, N., 91